DEDICATION

Dedicated to Violet Mary Leyfield
and Victor Frederick Henry Leyfield.

As loving parents, they have shaped my life.

CONTENTS

A WEALTH OF PENNIES

1. In a Slower Time — 001
2. Inside the Gate — 005
3. The Ones Who Came to Call — 009
4. Food For Thought — 013
5. Like One of the Boys — 019
6. Our Own Bit of Sky — 023
7. Red Letter Days — 027
8. A Bit of Green — 033
9. Are You Sitting Comfortably? — 037
10. Breaking Free — 041
11. A Cut Above — 045
12. She'll Pass if She Has a Good Day — 051
13. For There Are Those That Care — 057
14. But Am I Good Enough? — 063
15. An Easter I Once Knew — 067
16. Pink Christmas Bells — 071
17. First Love — 075
18. The Ladies From Stationery — 079
19. Always There – My Mum — 083
20. My Dad – A Man of Few Words — 089
21. The Day Thou Gavest — 093
22. The Wealth Of Pennies — 097

PREFACE

In 1991, my short story *My Dad – A Man of Few Words* was selected for *The Times* and *The Sunday Times* Cheltenham Literature Festival. This led to a tour with other writers, reading our work around libraries in Gloucestershire. From this, I wrote a series of 11 similar autobiographical stories for *Cotswold Life* magazine between 1991 and 1999, detailing my life in Gloucester as a child of the Fifties. In 2004 these stories along with several more were compiled in an anthology published by the *Daily Mail*. With that first edition now out of print, I'm thrilled to be able to present this newly updated version for a worldwide audience. I hope that in reading it you enjoy our time together.

Ann

IN A SLOWER TIME

I have only to close my eyes and I am back in Alfred Street again, playing hopscotch on the uneven slabs outside our house, muddy water splashing my socks. The rickety slabs were soon to be pulled out and replaced by smooth pavements where marbles and trolley wheels would run free. The street lamps were also changing. Gloucester's streets were being bathed in a warm, orange glow and with the new lamps one could see from one side of the street to the other, even on the darkest of nights.

Our house had a lamp outside, and it was so powerful you didn't need to put the front bedroom light on. This was the room where I was born on March 24th 1950. Mum and Dad had already had my brothers Roger and John. I was the baby of the family and it was from those windows Dad threatened to throw me, I just wouldn't stop crying – already I had too much to say!

I grew up in a world of red bricked houses. Ours was an end of terrace, saved from being right on the pavement by a small fence. We were glad to have a back alley access, useful when the coal man would come.

I didn't have a watch and I had no need for one, as I knew the time playing on the streets by the foundry siren at twelve and five o'clock. At these times there would be an exodus of men and women walking purposefully down the street to get home as quickly as they could. Many railwaymen travelled on their bikes to Horton Road Gates where my brothers train spotted, underlining in *Ian Allen* books, the great numbers of steam.

My mum worked in a clothes factory. She worked for many hours standing on her feet. All day she would snip ends the machinists had left behind and returned their mistakes. During the summer months when the windows were open, I could stand in the street and hear the clatter of the machines. *Music While You Work* had to be played so loudly if it were to be heard. It helped to take minds off tired feet and mouths cotton-dry from the dust.

I was nine when Mum started work. I resented it as I had no knowledge of how poor was a railwayman's pay and how hard it was to feed three children. All I knew was I now had to join the school dinner queue for thick stodge and lumpy custard and find the key in the greenhouse to let myself in at the end of the school day. The house was cold and quiet. I had to boil a kettle and put the potatoes on to cook before Mum was home at a quarter to five.

1. IN A SLOWER TIME

Although the house did have an old range, it was carefully hidden behind a curtain as Mum was proud of her new *Belling* cooker with two solid plates and a flat griddle. She had had many years of lifting pans and cooking on open fires and ranges as she was in service as a cook. Her culinary skills eked out the pennies to provide warm, nourishing meals on a large square, kitchen table. It was beautifully polished but the wood was never seen as it was covered by a red velvet cloth, ideal for card playing in the evenings. For every day use, it was covered by an oil cloth and for meals – a cotton check cloth as well!

Dad sometimes had a "lucky find," a rabbit or two would be hanging up in the "cubby-hole" - the cupboard under the stairs. Once I remember a mallard duck, hung by its feet, its wings splaying helplessly. The ring around its neck and the vivid colourful feathers were soon to be plucked away. I couldn't help but think that such a beautiful creature should be left to live.

To begin with we had no fridge. All the butter, dripping and any cold meat would be kept in a safe, a mesh covered cupboard on top of a cold stone shelf. We ate mainly fresh vegetables from Dad's allotment. If we were to have the luxury of chicken it would last almost a week – roasted, cold, then boiled with vegetables to make soup.

Every week an enormous earthenware bowl would be put on the table and soon there would be all the glorious smells of cinnamon, nutmeg, warm fruit cake and sweet sticky treacle tarts. I would play with the old weights on the scales and then I'd be given a tiny lump of pastry to make a jam turnover for my tea. The mangled monstrosity often leaked bubbling jam and made a mess of the baking tin. It was these first attempts that were to start me on a love affair with cooking to last a lifetime.

As I was the only girl in the family, I had my own room. I had stayed too long in my large cot by the side of Mum and Dad. I didn't want to move out. They tempted me by allowing me to choose my own paint and wallpaper. I chose pink flowers in squares and the paintwork was nursery blue. I slept on a cosy feather mattress with a stripy tick pillow. Smooth shiny lino was ice cold to my feet so bed socks were a must, a hand made rag rug at the side of the bed – sheer luxury!

That small room was to become a haven. First to line up my dolls, give them sheets of paper with ticks and teach them their tables, in true school practice. Later to lie gazing dreamily at a million pictures pulled out of *Jackie* magazine with all the 60s pop stars smiling at me from every inch of the wall. How I loved the secrecy of my room to read forbidden books like *Peyton Place*, or lie on a pillow damp with tears shed for a spotty boy who didn't know I existed.

Nowadays, when life seems too harsh or too fast, I like to think back to a slower, gentler time. I remember being lifted out of a tin bath in front of the fire, wrapped in a warm towel, feeling like a princess in her stole, and leaving my small wet prints on the bath time rug. My warmed nightie would be taken from the wooden clothes horse around the fire. As I dressed, Mum would be leaning over the fire with a long metal fork, toasting hot chunks of bread for my supper. This memory still warms me and makes me feel loved and secure. My only fear then would be Dad looking at the clock and pronouncing "up the wooden hill!" I knew there would be no argument, but if l stayed quiet, and said a very earnest prayer – perhaps bed would be postponed for a while, or at least until after the end of *Wagon Train*!

2. INSIDE THE GATE

INSIDE THE GATE

"Where is our Ann?"

I heard them, but I didn't budge. I was sitting on the back step, dusty knees up to my chin, tracing a groove in between the yard slates for the ants to run along. Sometimes I'd block their way with a stick or some grass, but they always got through – they won in the end. Rather like my lying low would make not a pennyworth of difference - I still had to go. All of us had to, or Mum and Dad could go to prison.

At first I was taken on the back of Mum's bike in a little metal seat, hard to sit on but I loved to hug her with my knees. One day, the back wheel had a puncture. The bang was so loud I thought we'd been shot. Looking at the sad flat tyre instead of a pool of blood, I sent up a prayer of thanks. Surely we couldn't go now? We did, and arrived late. Mum walked me in bubbling too many apologies.

The black iron spikes around the school yard were to keep us in. There was a finality about the rattling of the iron gate. The bell was rung. No more running – you walked in line to enter a carbolic-scrubbed sanctum of high arched windows and desks in rows ironed to the floor. They were all facing a lectern desk of Olympian height where Sir sat and peered down.

With hunched shoulders we started the blackboard crammed with a million sums. Sometimes we had a Composition Lesson. I remember three titles often written on the board: "The Journey of a Penny"; "The Adventure of a Postage Stamp" and "What I Did in the Summer Holidays". As Sir wrote each one I prayed for the next to spark some flame of interest – a really good title never came!

Most lessons were taken from old text books with much print, few pictures and many a dark finger print in the corner of the page. I pondered on the fact that many sad children had suffered the same lesson. Sometimes we read around the class. I would wait in turn for my name to be read out. When I'd muttered haltingly my allotted number of lines, I sighed with relief having no interest in the story. It seemed to me that teachers had only come across dull religious texts or lengthy descriptive classics. Didn't they know about the escapades of the *Famous Five* or *Smuggler Ben* and *The History of Cliff Castle*? I identified with George, the tomboy girl, who lived life dangerously on mysterious islands of adventure.

There was one magnificent factor about school life in the fifties – it was the silence. Speaking was idle chatter so

2. INSIDE THE GATE

"lips closed" became the order of the day. Soon I learnt no one could stop my mind. It was with this realisation I could break free from the religious murky picture in the corner of the room, the yellowed map of the world ripping at the corners, and the rows of milk bottles defrosting on the radiators. I could gaze up at the blue sky outside the arched windows and pretend I was not there. This became easy once a week in Nature Study. We would listen to the radio and in exquisite clarity, the *BBC* brought into our dusty old classroom, the sweet sound of a nightingale or the scratching of a mole. I was then whisked away to my own countryside, sitting on a railway sleeper, watching Dad plant potatoes in the black rich earth of his allotment.

We were told to finish our work quickly for the treat of the week – PE. On a concrete yard we learnt to do a forward roll on a raffia mat making its mark on bony shoulders. If I finished first I would wait for the others, idly poking a hole in my pinching daps or pulling a loose thread in the mat.

Painting was regarded as too messy but we did make *Plasticine* models. I would proudly make a family of people carrying baskets with tiny round eggs. These were squashed into a mashed lump with everyone else's at the end of the lesson.

I liked singing in the canteen. I would raise my voice to give what I thought of as a fair rendering of *Bobby Shafto* or *Sweet Polly Oliver*, and surreptitiously kicked and squashed peas left from school dinner. We dared to raise our bottoms half an inch as we sang, "Hooray and up she rises!" We sang many hymns. I remember - "the tall trees in the winter, the meadows where we play, the rushes by the water we gather every day." All of this had nothing to do with our terraced red-bricked roads, and even less with the formidable Victorian grey building where we were singing! Somehow just singing about them let a little of the

7

blue sky into our lives. I could sing it in my mind during dreadful Needlework, completing tiny drawn-thread stitches on a grey, once white, handkerchief. Needlework was to me a battle - the proof was the small round spots of blood, as somehow I was never quick enough to claim a much wanted thimble.

A bell began and a bell ended the day. It was the same bell – but the ring at four o'clock seemed a brighter, clearer sound. After the end of day prayer, we were dismissed. A dap bag was left swinging, a paper towel on the floor but I was out of the gate running away from the railings breathing my fill of the fresh clean air outside.

The strange thing is that when I got home I often lined up my dolls repeating the same lessons of the day. As a young child I was as strict as the teachers mimicking their words and actions. Gradually I stopped playing schools. Later I taught groups at *Girls Brigade* and *Sunday School*. I wanted so much to be a teacher, but not like my teachers. I vowed I would be kind and listen to my pupils, give them a chance at self expression, make learning more meaningful and fun, introduce them to a creative colourful world where they would have their right to challenge and discover. These are still my ideals. After many years in teaching I am still moved by the young faces in assembly as they sing their hymns. I wonder what dreams are held behind those earnest eyes. It's a breakthrough when one child looks my way – I wink, and they smile. Between us we're creating a little of that blue sky – inside the gate.

3. THE ONES WHO CAME TO CALL

THE ONES WHO CAME TO CALL

"You better move quick, our John. Mr Innes won't pay you for staying at home! Folks are relying on you."

Picking up his hunk of fruit cake and leaving half a cup of tea, he was off. He ran up the back alley not stopping until he got to Barton Street, where Mr Innes had packed the first load of groceries on his errand boy's bike. Each school day from half past four to six and on a Saturday morning he earned the princely sum of thirty bob a week. He was following in the footsteps of our older brother Roger, who was also an errand boy for *Fowler's Wines and Spirits*. How I envied their grand positions. As knights of the Gloucester roads, they were men of independent means! They were proud to belong to the battalion of the ones who came to call.

The whole week was peppered with callers who sold their wares and passed on the news. The milkman began the day. Two callers, who tottered carrying their cumbersome loads on a bike, were the window cleaner and the chimney sweep. How they managed to carry their heavy ladders or black, bristling brooms without falling off was a wonder. Cycling past, you gave them a wide berth!

Many of the callers just walked boldly down the back alley without bothering to knock. It was important to make sure your step was given the red *Cardinal* polish after the dustbin man had called. He would walk into your garden and collect the bin, lift it high up on his shoulders often dropping egg shells on the way.

The Rag and Bone man was for me a star attraction. He would certainly warrant getting out your trolley made from old pram wheels and with one knee on the ledge I'd scoot all the way up Alfred Street. His cart was pulled by a black and white cart horse. He'd yell, "Rag and Bone" and I'd yell with him, scooting hard to keep up with the cart to marvel at the brass bedsteads, blankets, old jumpers and pots and pans. He was a swarthy character with a glint in his eye – so unlike the coal man who frightened me. He wore a leather waistcoat which had worn smooth and shiny where he rested the sacks on his shoulder. Perhaps it was the strange hat with the leather piece around his neck and his coal dust ingrained face that unnerved me.

No one could fear the *Esso Blue* man in his neat little grey nylon overall. He drove a three wheeler van which sounded like a motor bike. He would open his back doors and we'd line up with our cans to be filled from a huge tank with a cartoon flame figure on the front. Most folks had a paraffin heater – I used to lean on ours with no worry about breathing in the fumes, only glad of the comfort of heat as I boggled over maths homework.

The highlight of the year was when the spring tides brought the elvers and the fishermen would ring a bell to sell their catch. It was always on a Sunday morning. The back of a cart would hold a large tin bath crammed full of

3. THE ONES WHO CAME TO CALL

the squirming worm-like creatures. They would sell them by the pint. I remember carrying home a jug of elvers doomed for the pan to be fried alive. I could never fancy them with an egg on bread – too similar to the bait that our John used for bream fishing down at Haw Bridge.

I remember an unexpected visit from the new vicar. Mum was horrified that the whole house stank of elderberry wine, for she and Dad had been boiling it up as it hadn't started to ferment. That wine caused some red faces before it was even drunk!

A welcome face was the *Wye Valley Pools* man. For a couple of shillings he gave you a dream that, just by chance, you could win the jackpot. My dad paid for years with no luck, yet my uncle joined for just three weeks and came up with a fair sum.

The people who came to call were important as they gave a shape to our week. Everyone knew the day for the Egg man, the Baker, the Insurance man. Folks would chat and messages were passed on. Each would help out those who would miss the callers and would show concern if perhaps, because of illness, someone hadn't answered the door.

It was the neighbourliness which built communities full of lively, caring people, glad to be served by the ones who came to call.

4. FOOD FOR THOUGHT

FOOD FOR THOUGHT

"As long as we have a roof over our head and enough for eat and heat – we'll be alright." This was my dad's simple philosophy and through the cold, hard, wet years working on the railway, he provided just that.

When he came through the door he would smell the meal cooking. Just within the time it took him to take off his heavy work jacket and boots, then lather his hands with cold water in the stone sink – it would be on the table. It was a piping meal, meat and two veg being the order of the day. No-one spoke until Dad had finished. I copied the way he ate his veg first, then the meat and as I took my last mouthful of treasured meat, he would wink and cut a small piece of his and put it on my plate.

A clean plate at the end of a meal was a duty; anything that was left, an insult or even worse – waste. Rationing had only just been lifted and I soon learnt it was better to swallow hard and get rid of the cabbage, than have the long lecture of how my "poor father" had worked his fingers to the bone on his allotment – just to see we were all well fed. Once my brother John refused to eat his greens and was told to stay at the table until he did. It grew cold, the gravy congealed. He was on his own, Mum was upstairs. Then she saw him out of the bedroom window, scraping his dinner into the dustbin. I shall not forget the blood-curdling scream and the forceful steps that stamped down the stairs. Cowering in the shed at the bottom of the garden he must have said some earnest prayers, as nothing was mentioned to Dad at the tea table that night. Some things, I learnt, were too bad to remember!

Often we waited to be excused from the table. To sit in silence was hard so I would end up tracing with my eyes the lines on the cloth, fingering its fraying edges in my lap and gazing at all the things that were always there. A loaf on a wooden board, large knife to the ready, the large brown tea pot and glass sugar bowl with clawed feet and the milk still in the bottle. We had a jug for when visitors came – Mum was always very embarrassed if we were caught with the bottle on the table. After we were excused, Mum and Dad would sit cradling their teacups, often not saying a word, just finding a bit of peace in the day.

For breakfast we all "went to work on an egg" stamped with a little *Lion*. We "dranka pinta milka day," just as the lady in the adverts told us - a third of a pint was provided

4. FOOD FOR THOUGHT

free at school. Apart from porridge I knew of no other cereals until much later. We had our first toaster in the sixties. It was a heavy, chunky machine and using the new sliced loaf, toast became a regular snack.

Dinner, until Mum started work, was served at midday. We often had a rabbit stew, stuffed heart, belly of pork, liver and onions, chips from the shop on Saturday and on a Sunday, always roast. Chicken was only for Christmas or Easter and steak never heard of! Puddings were glorious milky home-made bowlfuls of plenty. This was to fill you up and make up for the limited costly protein. The macaroni, tapioca, and rice puddings were warming. We had tarts and pies using fruits Mum had preserved in jars during the autumn. These were a treat but what we hated most were steamed suet puddings. Mum felt she was a connoisseur of these and we had them often. John and I had watched the *Ban the Bomb* marches on the television so we decided to follow their example.

We made banners and marched around our yard yelling, "Ban the steamed pud!" I can't remember Mum laughing so much and she got the message. No more Spotted Dick – we had won!

My favourite meal was 5 o'clock tea – bread, home-made plum jam, large chunks of hard ridged blue-rinded cheese with home-made tomato chutney. There was always fruit cake, mainly because Dad would have a piece daily in his tin for work with four cheese and chutney sandwiches wrapped in greaseproof paper.

No-one ate crisps as we were told these were costly snacks mostly sold in pubs. Chocolate biscuits were a luxury, perhaps a small packet kept for visitors, rather like the tin of peaches and artificial cream in case someone came unexpectedly for Sunday tea.

Although the food we ate was plain, Mum was very fussy about the china we used. No-one ever drank tea from anything but a matching cup and saucer and these would match with the plate, even if it were just a snack. There were several tea sets – everyday earthenware, next best more ornate earthenware for visitors and the gilt-edged, family heirloom, bone china set, kept in the cabinet waiting for the Queen to visit! Mugs were used only for "Hot Chocolate, Drinking Chocolate" or when we became one of the *Ovalteenie Girls and Boys*. Coffee was rarely drunk, although Dad did take a bottle of *Camp* for work. It was not until the sixties that instant coffee became popular, and we only regarded this as a mid-morning drink.

We bought biscuits mixed and loose from the large tin selection in the Maypole. This was my favourite local shop. I loved to watch the shopkeeper cut and pat the rich yellow butter and fold it so neatly in greaseproof. Thick sliced bacon was weighed on the small brass scales with much efficiency and accuracy. I shopped weekly for Mum at the *Maypole*. Its black and white floor, marble ledges and shiny brass counter bar I'll remember always.

In the butchers queue I made swirling patterns in the sawdust with my feet. I watched the heavy cleaver fall to chop the breast of lamb. If it were a piece for roasting he would cut fat and wrap it all up in white paper with the price of its contents written clearly on the corner.

Occasionally on the way home I would pop into Artus the watchmaker to leave an alarm clock to be checked or mended. The white-haired old man worked near the window. He knew Dad relied on his clock for shifts and he always lent Dad another until it was mended.

In the sixties came the first convenience food – fish fingers. It was thought to be a lazy wife's dinner – it was

4. FOOD FOR THOUGHT

too simple, too quick, so how could it be good for you and what a price! The height of laziness was to buy the new pre-cut crinkle oven chips when most people grew their own potatoes.

Ordinary people did not usually eat out. When my brother started earning and took Mum out, I remember her boasting to her friends she had had a meal not at a table, not even on a plate, but from a basket! Food such as curry, chilli, lasagne were just as foreign to us as frog's legs. Yet, we were to be the pioneers in trying these new foods while Mum and Dad ate as they always had and complained that food didn't taste the same.

The *Co-op* was where we collected milk and bread tokens and claimed our divvy. It was the first shop near us to become a supermarket. I rather liked the slow browsing and the freedom of pushing a trolley and shopping at your own pace. This was so much better than being tongue-tied at the counter. Soon the large hypermarkets were dreams being made into reality. The time of butter pats and sawdust on butcher's floors would soon be gone. I could not have imagined all the foods from other lands we now enjoy. Yet my family still like to sit around the kitchen table chatting about the day. In reality, not a great deal has changed. We continue to work hard to provide for "eat and heat" and take comfort cradling a cup of tea, still trying to find a bit of peace in the day.

LIKE ONE OF THE BOYS

"Have you finished those pots?"

"Yes Gran."

"Wiped, put them away?"

"Yes Gran."

"Top and tailed the goosegogs?"

"Yep – took me ages."

"You'll eat the tart just like everyone else."

"Can I go now?"

"If you see them brothers of yours, say 5 o'clock tea and give yourself time to wash the muck off you."

The creaky door to gran's two up two down was opening. I'd got past the cork mat, down the stone step and I was waving, running and the squeal of glee wobbled to the pounding of my sandals. I was gone.

Through Grandad's garden of sky-high veg and I was pushing the wooden gate and heading for the hill. I ran 'til my side hurt so I could look down on the row of cottages of Lyonshall. It was a peaceful, contained valley – green, dewy and the sunshine bathed on each grey, slate roof. This was a place for holidays and a million miles from the factories and foundry of Alfred Street where I lived.

This was where the dreaming began. I could sing *All Alone am I* and I was performing at the *London Palladium*. Thousands sat in their red tip-up seats. I was a star who moved them to tears. They stood to applaud. I was singing all that they felt.

I ran down the hill to the wood where the German girl with white hair lurked. I saw her once behind a tree, watching me. My brother called her rude names and it got back to Gran. The dark trees could mean ambush and I was not going to be found. I scratched a love heart and initials of a spotty boy who would never know of the Valentine I didn't send. Dreamily I collected teapots from the dump, kettles with burnt out bottoms and old green bottles speckled with murky mould. I lay crazy paving of pieces of best Sunday china around a blackened gas ring. It would never be lit again and yet it seemed to bring warmth to me as I stirred leaves in a pan sitting on an old tin bath.

There was a gunshot – I whispered "Rabbits!" and I was climbing again to the overgrown line. Soon I was jumping sleepers, watchful and wary of lizards under a sandalled foot, snakes in the bracken, socks caught and legs scratched by barbed wire. There was barbed wire that

5. LIKE ONE OF THE BOYS

twisted and turned and tried to keep out someone like me who still walked to Titley Station. I could never get into the building but just peered through a clear spot on the dusty window. There I saw an old railwayman's coat, dust clinging to the folds as it hung redundantly on a brass peg. Brown tufted pages of once needed timetables were scattered on the floor. A chipped, enamel mug had been left on the oak table next to a bunch of keys to once important places. I gazed down the weedy, once perfect platform and through the mist I could hear the screeching of brakes, the slamming of doors, the cries of welcome and the guard waving his flag shouting, "Titley, Titley!"

I wandered back to Grandad's garden and passed through the trellised archways of sweet peas flagged by regimental lines of carrots and cabbages. I would recite poetry, articulating, moving my head to nod and accentuate. The cabbages were my pupils hanging on to every word of wisdom that came from my lips.

At the bottom of the garden was a small chapel, large enough to sit twenty but I had never seen more than four go in. My great aunt pounded a hundred miles on a wheezy harmonium. A Bible clenching, straight backed woman sang of what a friend she had in Jesus and the congregation leaned on well polished pews, rubbed clean by a thousand best Sunday coats. The tired pews creaked as the congregation stood, sat, stood and sat once again.

Mum was calling. No sign of the boys. God help them if they're late. I walked back slowly dreaming of thin sliced bread and butter where you could see your fingers through the holes. My goosegogs will be in the tart but also there will be all the "hands in your laps", "don't talk while you're eating" and "sit still 'til you're excused" After waiting an age, then there will be the everlasting pots again! But Grandad will be there, big, smiley with his waistcoat pulling at the seams and his large rough hands dealing out the cards on the red, velvet cloth. We will play Spoof and he will tell tales of rooks going to school in the woods.

Mum and Gran will gossip as they sit in the rocking chairs either side of the hearth. At half past six the nine inch black and white *Bush* will be switched on for *Songs of Praise*. They will warble their *Abide With Me*'s and I will be content to be snuggled next to my dad, grandad and my brothers, playing cards as one of the boys, and a million miles from "women's work" and washing those pots.

OUR OWN BIT OF SKY

"Look at those rooks – have you ever seen birds in such a hurry to get back to the wood? They've all been to their different schools and are coming back to have bread and jam for tea."

We'd giggle at Grandad as he gazed out of the tiny panes of his cottage window.

"Trouble with you townies is you haven't got time or space. Look at all them folks we saw in Gloucester last Saturday. Well, I says to myself, where do they all go to sleep at night? I just couldn't live like it, crammed up in a town."

He told us tales of rooks who busied themselves with learning but still found time to gaze at their own bit of sky. He felt sorry for us children living in an unhealthy place with sooty railways, an iron foundry and row upon row of red-bricked terraces. He admitted the schools were good and children had more of a chance to get on "learning-wise," but did they know what they were missing?

It didn't matter if it was Grandad's small paned windows or the wooden sash ones in Alfred Street – the sky for me was the same all over. Rich and poor, country bred or townie, weren't we all entitled to our own bit of sky and time to gaze from out of our own window? I'd sometimes catch my Mum doing just that. I'd sidle in and she would put her arm around me and carry on gazing. If she spoke, it nearly always was to kiss the top of my head and to say how lucky we all were, and we knew it. At that moment the sky could have been grey and bleak but my soul was warmed by her nearness.

There were times when fear crept into Mum and Dad's voices. This was when illness was mentioned. In the Fifties good health did not seem so much a right as a stroke of good fortune. "Your health is everything," Mum would say. She had had diphtheria as a child and knew what it was like to be quarantined from her family. A father ill could mean no pay and the family on the bread line. I remember hearing hushed voices whispering of a railwayman friend being "on the panel." The *National Health Service* had been introduced for several years but old expressions and attitudes lingered.

We certainly didn't visit the Doctor often. Home remedies sufficed – cod-liver oil, a spoonful of *Virol* every day, *Veno's* cough mixture and Vicks *VapoRub*, *Aspro* and *Milk of Magnesia* were always at hand. My Doctor's surgery had a paint peeling conservatory and weeds growing in a gravel path. The waiting room was huge and cold. There were large leather arm chairs, well worn with holes where sprigs of stuffing scratched your wrists. Everything was dusty, airless. There was a pile of well-thumbed *National Geographic* magazines. Patients sat in huddles. The sounds were the familiar coughs of pleurisy, bronchitis and, hopefully not what everyone feared, TB.

6. OUR OWN BIT OF SKY

I was frightened of spit. Don't go near it. Don't share another person's teaspoon, you never know… A teacher licked her finger to alter a sum on my slate. The wet stain worried me. Germs hid, you couldn't be sure.

The Polio epidemic meant our weekly trip to the Swimming Baths came to a stop. We were all wary from seeing on *BBC News*, row upon row of poor children in their iron lungs.

We hadn't the confidence that antibiotics bring today. Penicillin and M&B drugs were used but not as readily. Doctors still kept ointments and made up linctuses as you waited. Rest, warmth and good food were often prescribed. Mums practised home nursing, rocked poorly children through the night, tepid water sponging to bring down the fever. There was much faith put in clear soups and egg custards. My aunt brought my mum a bottle that promised to really "buck you up" – *Sanatogen Tonic Wine*.

We were hounded by the usual childhood illnesses, but everyone feared whooping cough and scarlet fever.

When I was nine, the Doctor came to our house to see Mum. I knew she must be very ill – no-one called the Doctor unless it was serious. She lay grey and limp but still managed to give me a smile. The Doctor said I was to be very brave and become "Chief Nurse." I promised him earnestly that I would keep a sharp eye on Mum if Dad was at work. I would make sure she had food and drink and she stayed in bed.

Mum said she wanted a thin slice of bread and butter. I had asked, "Only one?" She insisted, only the one, so I cut her a huge slice, at least an inch thick and with almost as much butter. I remember her watery smile when she saw the huge lump presented on her best china. I remember warming some rice pudding for her and, as her face screwed up taking the first mouthful, I realised I'd burnt it. At that point the chief nurse forgot to be brave. I cried as I flopped on her bed. She patted my bowed head and said it really wasn't that bad.

Many Doctor's visits and many prayers later she slowly got better and the absolute joy of seeing her out of bed and in her flowery apron once more was worth all the Christmases and birthdays rolled into one.

I could gaze again from a simple town house window. Now Mum was well, I saw a vista of blue pools, white soft billowing mountains with pink-edged hidden empires. It was a warm smiling sky where rooks once more could fly home to their woods to eat bread and jam for tea.

RED LETTER DAYS

Mum and Dad were a true love story. Their favourite song was "I know I'll never find another you." I'm not saying they didn't have their disagreements, but in front of the children, they were a united front. Dad loved football and when I was very young he played in a local team. Mum was not pleased at being left alone during their precious free time so his only game was to be on TV – *Match of the Day*. Mum said the only good thing about the programme was the introductory music. I loved to sit next to him as he watched. I can still hear his oohs as some one just missed such an easy goal!

He showed his fancy footwork when he played football with my cousins on Minchinhampton Common. Dad's brother Mervyn and his wife Belinda and children Roy and Barry were there. They had travelled on their motorbike and side car. We had arrived in RDF (our car's number plate). It was Dad's first, and only, brand new car. It was a 1956 blue *Ford Prefect* with a "pudding stirrer" gear stick, 3 gears and no synchromesh.

Sometimes he would crunch the gears or stall and he would say, "Darn that kangaroo petrol!" I wondered why he didn't buy another kind!

How he loved that car. It was always kept so clean and well polished. Dad rented a garage in Birchmore Road and once a week it came out to do the regular visits to Lyonshall and Oaksey.

Oaksey is a small village near Kemble in Wiltshire. It was where Dad was brought up. In a school drawing book he drew Oaksey Halt. This is a bridge over a railway line, where the trains in those days stopped. He lovingly drew every brick. The heart of Oaksey is the church. In that graveyard lay several Leyfields. The most important and precious to him was his mother, Amanda. She died when I was very young. It was in that church the family celebrated and cried at christenings, weddings and funerals.

There is a special road in Oaksey called Bendybow. It was there Dad's father, his sister Peg, her husband Cliff and their nine children lived, also Mervyn and his family. There was his younger brother, Fred and his wife Audrey and their family who lived in a nearby village. As with all my relations, they often visited us in Gloucester.

7. RED LETTER DAYS

It was on a Sunday we would visit Oaksey and this quiet village showed me a very different way of life compared to the rows of red-bricked houses and concrete pavements of Alfred Street. I was aware of a wider, larger sky when I visited Oaksey or Lyonshall. I loved to play with my cousins and enjoyed the smiling welcome and super teas! On Christmas Eve we all would meet up at Aunty Peg's house and Grampy would give out a present to each of the children. It's a tradition that still continues and Uncle Cliff is now the Grampy.

I was aware how lucky my cousins were to live in the countryside, miles from a foundry or factories. Mum and Dad were both country bred and it showed in their straight forward philosophies of life. They had made a decision to move to Gloucester for Dad's work. Dad also believed that his children would have more educational opportunities in a city. In those days, this was probably right. If I had lived in the countryside I am sure I would never have passed the 11+ as a country girl needed a higher mark than the city girls. The few country girls that made the grammar school were mostly in the A stream and extremely clever!

As we forfeited fields, peace and space of the countryside, Mum and Dad made sure holidays were spent out of town. We visited Lyonshall for the Easter holiday and for three weeks during the summer holidays we travelled all the way to Hayle in Cornwall. A man, who worked with Dad, owned a chalet called Glen View. Dad paid weekly rent for those three weeks. Mum called visits, and holidays "Red Letter Days" and we all loved them.

I remember now bracken whipping my legs as I ran down sandy ribboned paths of the Dunes. Hayle had golden sands. We travelled by train using a free pass and the endless journey was worth it. As a child, I thought

Cornwall was the absolute furthest place one could travel to! We were lumbered with heavy bags of not only clothes but vegetables from Dad's allotment. A taxi ride from the station was a once in a year treat. As I was the youngest, I had to sit on the hard pull out wooden seat while the more privileged enjoyed the well worn leather ones.

Glen View was only one of a host of chalets dotted about the hilly dunes. Sometimes entertainment was provided. I remember parades and fancy dress competitions. One year I wanted to go as a beauty contestant in my brand new swimming costume in the fancy dress. Instead I was dressed with my clothes facing the wrong way and everything back to front and I carried a placard "Backward Child." I did quite well in the competition. It gave a few laughs, but I was not amused!

Over the years we became friendly with the family in the next chalet. One year I remember their car arriving late at night. I was in bed and peeped from behind the curtains. The girl was the same age as me and I was longing to see her again. Her father later came to knock at our door. I heard sad, low voices. Something awful had happened. The mum had died and he had brought the children on his own. As Mum told me I didn't cry. It was just too awful to imagine. How could you live without a mum? Would you look different if your mum died? I asked Mum what I would say to her. She said not to say anything, just be friendly, just the same. The next day I went up to her quietly, awkwardly.

She said, "My mum died you know."

"Yes, I know," was my reply.

We went on playing together but the golden sands turned grey for a while.

7. RED LETTER DAYS

We all loved the vans that arrived outside the chalets. Their horns would blow and the children would come running. There was the daily baker's van and the newspaper van. There were also two lorries. One emptied the bins and the other was "the smelly lorry." We would run away holding our noses as the men in that lorry emptied the toilets!

I felt such a comfort squashed round the table of Glen View. The room was lit by a gas lamp and we would play cards and tell the stories of the day. We would drink warm sweet tea from Glen View's pretty primrose cups. Even if we were listening to the patter of raindrops on the chalet roof, no one worried, we were all together. For a while there were no shifts for Dad, no factory work for Mum and school belonged to another world. We were safe. We were together, making memories that would warm us for ever. These special times we called "Red Letter Days".

A BIT OF GREEN

"Oh Mum not again – it was only done last week."

"You leave it another week and there'll be more to cut."

"Why can't we have a mower like other folks?"

"'Cause I've got two galloping lads like you who are big enough and ugly enough to get on with it! Half hour with the shears and it'll be done. You don't expect your Dad to start after a hard shift."

Then it would start – the regular clip, clip, clip mixed with a few choice words as the six foot square was shorn. As I was a girl, I was exempt from this manly duty – but no one loved that small plot more than I. It was the only bit of grass we had and to me it was our countryside - just a bit of green. Surrounded by next door's shed and a low fence to divide our back yard from the rest of the garden - it was our most precious spot. So small a spot couldn't be called a lawn, lawns were part of rich folk's estates. We just called it "the grass."

It was on "the grass" that the family snapshots were taken. We had one of my older brother, Roger with his first new push bike. He bought himself a mirror for it. He was so thrilled to be able to see behind himself – he drove straight into a lamp post! The rest of us had to make do with second-hand bikes.

As I look back in the family album I can see us all in our Sunday best and just combed hair grinning back at Dad steadying his box *Brownie* camera. We'd all just fit in the small plot. Sometimes when visitors came they would sit on our two deck chairs. The grass would then be full, anyone else would have to perch on the coal bunker or the hard concrete path.

Many discussions and decisions were made over a cup of tea, sitting on those chairs. I preferred it when I was all alone and I had the grass to myself. On hot sunny days I could lie back and see just the blue dome above, then close my eyes and pretend this wasn't Alfred Street grass but perhaps sharper, coarser blades interspersed not with black, town earth but the soft shifting sands of the dunes. Within moments I would be whisked away to Hayle in Cornwall – the spiky grass hurting my legs as I ran to find a hiding place amongst the sharp ferns, my face licked by a soft sea breeze.

8. A BIT OF GREEN

It was on the grass at home that my messy play took place. I could never be trusted with mixing my flour and paint potions indoors. I would while away hours pasting pictures in scrap books. I remember secretly picking up fallen rose petals and stirring them in jam-jars of water to make perfume for Mum's birthday. The delicate "rose-water" often turned to a yellow stench as it waited to mature and then a home-made card with some freshly picked wild flowers would have to suffice.

It was strange how within that neat little town garden we all had peaceful times. Mum would often have a wistful look as she smoothed a white cotton sheet on the line. Dad would always be tending his plants in the greenhouse. My younger brother John would earn a penny a bucket, stoning. This was sieving the earth and leaf mould to produce a soft, velvet soil-rich and fine enough for the baby seedlings that Dad nurtured. I marvelled at Dad's great patience as he picked out each tiny green shred, planting them so neatly in rows. There were asters, petunias, marigolds and stocks – all carefully watered by a fine spray and kept in the greenhouse until the sign went up in our front window. Then a stream of people would be walking down our back alley to buy the plants. Dad would wrap each dozen in newspaper, just like fish and chips.

Sometimes a boy would come with a couple of pence for only two – he would send him away with a kind word and a few extra plants!

Of course our little bit of grass wasn't hilly with rough, dark dales and leaf-laden floors like the magical woods of Cranham. Neither was it far reaching and undulating with the velvet-smooth golf pitches and yellow winding paths of Painswick Beacon. We didn't have the vast landscape chequered with a hundred greens as seen from the top of Haresfield. These were special places kept for sunny

Sunday picnic days of daisy chains and a *Primus* stove that wouldn't light in a breeze. These were days of sounding notes on thick blades of grass between your fingers and counting the hours from a dandelion clock.

Back in our garden, space was at a premium and I was thankful for that six foot square of grass. In the summer this peaceful plot was given a colourful border of Dad's flower plants. While watching the bees fly from one bloom to the next I felt proud that a little bit of our garden was being shared with a hundred other railwaymen or foundry workers and neighbours. They were all just ordinary Gloucester folk who, like us, wanted a bit of colour to brighten their red-bricked yards and small grassy patches… for wasn't everyone entitled to a peaceful place? – their own "bit of green."

ARE YOU SITTING COMFORTABLY?

When the going was rough, I couldn't get a word in edgeways and not one person in the world understood – it was a haven, instant escape.

I could sit gazing at the white flaky distemper and trace the parts which had been picked off by fidgety fingers. Flesh coloured shapes were revealed. One was a silhouette of *Alfred Hitchcock*, the other an outline of Africa. Of course there were the dark spots – a black crevice where I had once seen the mother and father of all eight-legged creatures. It certainly hadn't been squashed by feeble me, so presumably still may live!

There was a gap under the door, three inches high, where you could sometimes see the rain pounding on the concrete step. It was those days you counted your blessings. Everyone in the row had one but at least ours was joined to the house and not in a shed at the bottom of the yard. No, ours was a brick built affair - *Twyfords* utility white cistern with a long chain pull. The flush was so immensely loud that as you pulled it, you took off fast, and waited by the back door for Niagara to calm to a trickle, before sneaking back to check that you'd left the door on the latch, so it didn't come off its hinges in the wind.

This was a spring and summer place. It was where much careful thought was churned over and many a tear shed. Privacy was at a premium and it was the one place no one bothered me. I could close my eyes and listen to Mum banging the rugs on the washing line, Dad shovelling a scuttle full of coal next door, our wind-up gramophone playing *Tommy Steele's Singing the Blues*, and I was on the throne swinging my legs and no-one at that moment was making any demands on me.

It was a different story in the winter. The white-washed retreat became a dark place of shadows. You needed a torch. The hairs on my legs stood on end and prickled just as if my eight-legged friend were taking a walk. Oh yes, the winter visits were sharp and quick. I often tried to avoid them by crossing my legs tight as I happily watched the last part of *Beat the Clock*.

I had to admit we were lucky with our modern facility. A visit for necessities at my Grandad's cottage was a different matter. It was an *Elsan* in a large wooden outhouse. There was a smell of chickens and corn in the dark. You either forfeited decency and left the door open and sang loudly or, with it shut, stared at the thin white crack beneath and hurried. Dark shadows of odd religious pictures were on the walls and a formidable embroidered tapestry of "Clothes Maketh the Man" preached at all who entered.

We, like Grandad, had newspaper on a string. It was a Saturday job for me to cut it into squares and thread it with a large tapestry needle. It hurt your fingers trying to get the hole central. I liked our squares better than Grandad's as ours often had interesting extracts. I was not

9. ARE YOU SITTING COMFORTABLY?

allowed to read newspapers as a child, but often read these squares - trying to match odd bits of information about the *Profumo Affair* with half a sequence of *Andy Capp*.

It was with much sadness and trepidation that I heard we were going to claim something called a "grant" – a magical amount of money to build a bathroom and toilet actually inside the house. We had had a few little changes done: sash windows were replaced by metal push out ones; the cabinets either side of the fireplace had been taken away as "old fashioned"; the black-leaded range had been removed and the fireplace replaced by a marble tiled affair. I just couldn't believe the old tin bath on the back wall would never be used again. No more Sunday baths in front of the fire on the clippy mat with my nightie warming on the clothes horse.

The builders came and chipped away the red-brick wall and soon a sparkling bath and washstand with silver taps was in its place. I was introduced to the low-level flush. I couldn't believe just a little push down and it would really work! It was a gentle gushing sound, no more the clank of Niagara – the flesh-coloured shapes gone forever.

I took a while to get used to the change. Neighbours came to marvel at the modern wipe-clean facility, but for me, there was now little escape. I could no longer pretend not to hear as they yelled that I hadn't finished the washing up.

My world was changing fast. Even our tiny new *Bush* television had the extra *ITV* channel. How wonderful those adverts – you could now pop out for the necessities without missing anything. Come winter nights I felt happier about our new addition. No more furtive glances beyond the torchlight. No breezes cutting below the door and no more tingling of hairs on my legs – I never did find out if it was my eight legged friend, and now I never will.

BREAKING FREE

I hated Saturday mornings. No lie in. Up early, quick breakfast, washtub pulled out and water heating ready. Many people chose Monday to do their washing, but now that Mum was at the factory, Saturday was a blitz of work.

At first it was the large heavy pans on the stove that were boiled to pour into the stone sink. In the same soapy water we washed whites, the colours and eventually, work clothes. Cold water was not metered, so much rinsing went on and then there was the carrying of wet, heavy clothes to the outside wringer. John got his fingers stuck in it once, how he screamed. It was really hard to push round the heavy handle, particularly when drying the thick twill sheets. They magically came out as a flattened sausage and then there was the difficulty of getting them on the wiped clean line without dropping an end in the earth. Really it was only on the centre of our small line that would do and even then, the sheets got caught on the rose bushes.

Later Mum reaped the benefit of working to be a proud owner of a *Hoover Twin Tub*. I remember the rubber pipe that emptied the used water. It gave out after the wash, water that was grey, slimy and still warm. This didn't go down the plug – too precious! It was used to fill a bucket and on my knees I would wash the front step and the multi-coloured floor tiles outside the front door. When the water was almost black it was gently poured on the pavement and then with a hard brush the outside pavement was scrubbed. It used to amuse me to see the wet line between the neighbours who bothered to do this and those that didn't.

There was such a pride on how the front of the house looked. I regularly cleaned the bay windows. The bottom pane was frosted. It had been replaced during the war as it had shattered after a bomb had dropped in nearby Derby Road. I hated red *Cardinal* polish under my nails as I learnt what elbow grease was as I attacked the front step.

The washing was safely on the line. There was a set routine. Sheets, shirts and trousers in the centre and dusters made from holey vests and all underwear were dried in the back yard, away from neighbour's view. Knickers were bunched up, so unlike our next door neighbour's who, instead of our cotton boilable knickers, wore black and red nylon scanties. They were blowing confidently for all to see. One day, I hoped I would wear such frillies!

Saturday meant cleaning the brass from the mantelpiece with *Brasso*. I didn't like the smell or the job assigned to me. There was hand bell with a Devon pixie on the top. There were several plates – one of Cockington Forge and the largest with the late King's head. My favourite was the brass horse letter rack which was emptied weekly of letters and bills. I also cleaned the cutlery with *Silvo*. It was important to wash these well afterwards or the polish would taint your food.

10. BREAKING FREE

To make life a little more bearable I would listen to *Family Favourites* on the radio. It was on a Saturday cleaning session I first heard *Please Please Me* by *The Beatles*. I was mesmerised by the different sound. I knew it would be a moment I would always remember. I was so glad to be part of the mania that was caused by the "fab four." I idolised *John Lennon*. How I admired his moody brashness and confidence. Roger's *Dansette* player played their records until almost their grooves were flat! *With the Beatles* and *Revolver* were my favourites.

The boys were not involved in this massive clean up on a Saturday as John was an errand boy and Roger, after being an errand boy, went on to be a voluntary police cadet. As in many times in my childhood, I wished I had been born with the advantages of being a boy!

I had been taught at an early age to iron – hankies at first, thick ones, not Sunday best lace-edged ones. I took an ironing test at *Girls' Life Brigade*. I lost marks when I ironed the centre of an apron, as I should have ironed the ties first! Later I was taught to iron a shirt and fold it, just like when it was new in the box. As soon as I could do this I had loads to do. I didn't mind the school shirts but hated Dad's check thick ones, often with frayed collar and cuff. The very worst were Roger's police shirts. They were not that difficult, but he was so fussy and always criticising as he "bulled" his boots and brushed his jacket.

Twelve o'clock I was sent to Gregory's chip shop. Mum and Dad had a fish between them and we had fish cake or meat patties – such luxury! After a meal with no washing up it was freedom for me. I was given five shillings pocket money and by the age of fifteen I was allowed to go to town. I bought my own stockings. They laddered so easily but I hated wearing socks. Then I would buy secret make up and wear it to attract the boy called Malcolm who

43

played the organ in church. Dad caught me once and I had to wash it off. He'd said, "Fancy being a painted woman to go to church!"

When I was fifteen I loved to sit in the *Wimpy Bar* drinking black coffee. I didn't like it but thought it made me look interesting! I leaned on record booths listening to *The Beatles* or *Cliff*. I couldn't afford the 45s any more than the minis and tall boots I longed for in the boutiques, but with a free squirt from a counter sample of *Channel No 5*, I was truly living and a million miles from *Persil*, *Pledge* and *Brasso*!

One day I did afford those short skirts and plastic boots. I had managed to hide my age and get a job as a Saturday girl at a large department store. The Saturday blitz was over for me.

Selfishly I didn't worry that now Mum would have to do more. I had escaped. Mum said surely Saturday mornings had not been that bad? I replied that even if they didn't pay me I would rather be a Saturday shop assistant! The freedom and independence were intoxicating. I vowed one day, instead of cotton boilables, I would wear black frilly nothings and they would dance and billow on the line without a care in the world, for everyone to see!

A CUT ABOVE

There is excitement in the air as wide, watchful eyes wait for it to begin. There is popping and banging from those who have started before and then there is a whoosh and a cascade of white, pink and yellow stars falling in the black sky. As each are lit we see the same as every year: a Roman candle, a traffic light, a Catherine wheel, some rockets.

The children are writing their names with sparklers, and I am taken back to a small blue slate yard not far from where I lived. I can remember my dad trying to persuade the wheel to turn on a rusty nail that stayed on a post for many years. We watched and stood well back and, framed by a trellis archway of honeysuckle, the magic took place.

I am not sure when it started. Both families were not well off so it was decided to share what fireworks we had to give a better display. It was the very one time of the year we were invited into the back garden, not the house. I was afraid of Mr H. He stood back, nodded, but didn't speak. "He thinks he's a cut above," Mum had said. He was one of the few white collar workers in the area. Not that it did him much good. Mrs H had let it slip how she had less meat to go round than we had.

I would be in last year's best coat, so thick, too tight, pulling across my chest and a large expanse of arm showed between my glove and sleeve as I showed little Mary how to draw with a sparkler. I was always bossy to her but she followed me everywhere and mimicked all I did.

Her little brother Marky was very different and everyone knew it. He was thin, small and stood apart. In all the years that I knew him, I never saw him smile. He made no friends. As other children walked to school he would walk on his own on the opposite side of the road. Mary was ordinary enough but little Marky, with his nose in the air, was like his dad – "a cut above."

I remember when I was about thirteen years old that Mum had given me one of her old lipsticks. Mary was in utter admiration as I pouted my red smudged lips. Marky must have been about six and the only words I ever remember him saying were, "Girls who wear lipstick have babies before they're married." Incensed I told John who went into tucks of laughter. Mum just paused, furrowed her brow and muttered, "I wonder where he got that from." I was told abruptly to wash it off and get ready for tea.

The bonfire ritual went on for several years. We took it in turn whose garden we went to. It was always strange to feel the silent stares of Mr H and Marky as they stood well back on their own.

"They're just odd and feel they're better than us," is what Mum would whisper.

I sensed a cold silent power and noticed how Mrs H would obey her husband without question.

11. A CUT ABOVE

Every couple of months Mrs H's mother would come to stay. She came from Yorkshire and I loved her accent. She had a moth-eaten tartan blanket around her shoulders and walked very painfully with a knotted wooden stick. She smelled of stale *Lily of the Valley* and a mousey mustiness. She was so kind and when she came to our house I would sit next to her knee and she would stroke my hair. To me, she was the wonderful granny that I needed.

She used to sniff snuff. Mum used to buy it for her. Her daughter did not approve and neither did they approve of the milk stout mum bought for when she came to visit. She came on a Monday and a Wednesday evening when she was in Gloucester. It was a couple of hours break from the front room of her daughter's house. She was an avid watcher of *Coronation Street* and with her broad friendly accent she was to me part of that street, just like *Ena Sharples* or *Minnie Caldwell*. Our house, as she slowly sipped her stout, became "the snug" of *The Rovers Return* pub. When she went back she always had a watery, grateful smile as I kissed her pale, silvery cheek. Then things started going very wrong.

She was unable to cope in her own home in Yorkshire so it was decided that half of the year would be spent with her daughter in the North and the other would be with the daughter in Gloucester. There must have been a row and Mrs H no longer looked after her mother. She was left alone in that front room with just a commode. Gradually the commode was not emptied and meals not provided. Mum was worried and waited for Mrs H to go out shopping. The front door was left open so she emptied her commode, provided meals and water, all apparently without Mrs H knowing, but mum felt she knew. I was in on the secret as I collected dinner plates and offered meals to her through the front window. Dad was furious and wanted to go round and make a big fuss. He said it was cruelty. Mum said we could make matters worse, and perhaps she wouldn't be able to get any help then.

Then it became the time to go to the other daughter from the North. Although we hated to see her go, we were relieved she would be at last looked after properly. I remember the tearful goodbyes and the hope in that dear old lady's eyes that things would get better. We waved as she started her long journey home.

In the middle of that night there was a knock at the door. It was a taxi driver. My dear old lady had arrived in Yorkshire and they didn't want her. She had returned to the cruelty of the other daughter and Mr H would not allow her over the threshold. On a cold winter night Dad asked her to come in. She was weary and cold. She gladly hugged Mum's hot water bottle and drank a hot drink. Dad, in his pyjamas, was tamping mad. Even now she would not say a word against either daughter but shook her head saying, "You don't know the half of it!" We had no spare room so Dad ran down to the phone box and rang the police. They were kind to her and went to appeal to Mr H but it was no good.

She was sent to an old peoples' home a couple of miles out of Gloucester. I don't know who paid for it, but it wasn't for long. I visited her. It seemed pleasant and clean. There was a television. I wanted to ask her if she watched *Coronation Street*, but she had changed. She was absolutely expressionless. Mum handed her some snuff and a couple of bottles of stout. She nodded thanks but after that, it was as if she was not there. She wasn't ill but she soon died. Mum said it was from a broken heart.

I don't remember ever going to their house again and we grew up and there were no more fireworks. Several years later we moved away and we met a neighbour who told us

11. A CUT ABOVE

that Mr H had been in trouble. It had been in the paper. It was something about fraud and for years he had kept two families and hadn't been married to Mrs H. We were glad to hear Mary was well. She had married an airman and moved abroad. Marky was found to be a person of extreme intelligence and within a top university had retreated into research.

The popping and the whizzing have finished. There are just a few stray rockets. The chill of the air has caused me to hurry in to a warm drink and to close the door. I find myself humming the theme from *Coronation Street*. I can see her watery smile and she is saying cheers as she raises her glass of milk stout.

(The names of the characters have been changed)

Post Script

Many years later I remember regularly my son Sam calling out saying, "Mum, *Corrie* is on," and we would snuggle up enjoying the programme together. Even in the difficult years when a teenager finds it hard to chat with his mum, *Corrie* was something we could talk about. One day I took him to *Coronation Street*'s *Granada Studios*. It was a day of much excitement and happiness. We met *Percy Sugden* and *Ken Barlow* and walked the famous street where the adventures we had shared had taken place.

We often could not afford fireworks so Sam would have a little pocket money and instead, sit on the window ledge of his bedroom with me and we would watch other peoples' fireworks as we munched a favourite tea. Recently Sam telephoned me from a firework display he was enjoying with his children. He said,

"Do you remember sitting on the window ledge watching fireworks together?"

Oh yes, I will always remember. These were such warm, happy, close times and I was so glad he remembered them. He and his wife will create happy memories for his children and the warmth of good times can carry on.

12. SHE'LL PASS IF SHE HAS A GOOD DAY

SHE'LL PASS IF SHE HAS A GOOD DAY

I was eleven years old. It had seemed just an ordinary school day until we arrived and realised this was it. I had to pass or I would never have a hope of becoming a teacher, and it was all I ever wanted to be. It was the 11+ exam which would determine whether I got to a grammar school. Just before we went in to take the Arithmetic paper Sir wrote a hasty "%" on the board. He told us not to touch that sum as we hadn't covered that work. This did nothing for my confidence! We had been primed for months just for this day. My mum was told, "If Ann has a good day, she'll pass." Well I was praying it was a really good day!

My maternal grandmother had never really liked me. When we arrived at her cottage at Lyonshall she would throw her arms open to welcome the boys, but not for me. Dad was always ready to pick me up for a cuddle as he saw I was hurt. They told me it was because she had had only one little boy and he had died, so she liked little boys. This was not my fault and I resented the way she treated me as a maid and not as a granddaughter. My Dad's mother had died and this was the only gran that I had left. I felt that she had let me down.

Gran suffered from petit mal fits and I remember being on a bus to do the shopping at Kington and she was just staring at me. It was a cold immovable stare. I still feel uneasy if someone stares at me now. I so wanted to impress Gran. On the morning that I received the letter to say I was accepted for the grammar school I couldn't wait to tell her I was the first member of the family to achieve this. I would at last make her proud of me. But she died before I could tell her the news. She let me down again! I can remember Mum hugging me and crying. I thought why is she getting so upset? It wasn't as if she was that nice! As an adult, I am sad now how often black and white and so unforgiving were my views as a child.

I was so proud to have passed the exam. My best friend, Julie also passed. We had been at school together since my first day at school. I was thrilled she would go to the new school with me. I was excited but also very worried. Would I manage? Would I keep up? Much extra plum picking in addition to extra night shifts would be needed for the costly uniform and a second-hand bike to get there. Roger was the only one to have a new bike. He smashed it into a lamp post because he was admiring himself in his new mirror, so after that John and I had to make do with second-hand ones!

12. SHE'LL PASS IF SHE HAS A GOOD DAY

It was a brand new building and really a great beginning because Julie and I were as lost as the teachers and the older girls. The grammar school was very different. We had debating societies and for perhaps the first time in my school life I was asked my point of view. We even had mock elections. Dad primed me for voting *Labour* and I learnt his expressions without really understanding what they meant. I remember when *Winston Churchill* died. I watched his state funeral. Everyone at school told us of his great life. I spoke of him with reverence to Dad. He raised an eyebrow and said "What about the Welsh?" I offered this gem at school and felt a right lemon when questioned what did I mean? I hadn't a clue!

Most years we went to Stratford to see a Shakespearian play. I am sad to say I don't remember any of them. I was just too young. Then a new, enlightened English teacher called Mrs Croke thought it a good idea to visit Stratford's *Royal Shakespeare Theatre* just to look around the empty building. It was superb! We tiptoed into dressing rooms that *Elizabeth Taylor* and *Richard Burton* had used. We saw a parade of photographs of stars. I marvelled at the row of elegant costumes in the wardrobe department. The most wonderful part was being allowed to walk one by one on to the stage and to quote some *Shakespeare*. I didn't need to be asked twice. I called out "To be or not to be, that is the question" and the words rebounded at me from all around, not needing a microphone. I imagined all those empty seats full and the audience clapping, just for me. To this day I love to perform – to act, sing and tell stories. What an opportunity to be on one of the most important stages of the world. Thanks for the memory Mrs Croke.

While I was at the grammar school, man got to the moon. We were shown the films at school and told this time was making history. Somehow it didn't impress me as much as *Beatlemania* which crept into our lives and overtook us like a storm. I also had a worry closer to home – a bully, Linda. She had fuzzy hair and the current fashion was long straight hair like *Sandie Shaw*. I had long straight hair and that was the problem. She would tease me asking how often did I wash my hair and also tirelessly mocked me about my weight. I used to wash my hair before school and cycle with it damp for two miles so that Linda wouldn't say it needed washing. She was always in trouble and I was mainly a "goody two shoes." This changed one day when something exploded in me.

It was lunch time. I sat round a table of eight girls and Linda was opposite. The group started to discuss Speech Day, when we were allowed to go to the dance as a non-uniform day. I was not fat but certainly not thin and everyone in those days longed to look like *Twiggy*. We were finishing our pudding – something and custard. Another table had plonked a dish cloth in front of me, ready to wipe our table at the end of the meal. They hadn't rinsed it. I could see the custard and squashed peas in its folds. Then Linda began:

"What are you wearing to Speech Day?"

"I don't know," I mumbled, chin on chest.

"My sister is just like you. Poor thing, all her clothes are like tents!"

An enormous power came upon me. I stood up, picked up the messy cloth and walked slowly to her. To this day I can feel the mass of curly hair in my left hand as my right as hard as I could, smothered the custard and peas into her face. I stopped suddenly. Fear took hold and I ran from the dining room. She ran after me screaming. The teacher on duty only saw her and called out demanding she went to sit out side the headmistress' office.

12. SHE'LL PASS IF SHE HAS A GOOD DAY

I heard it all and hid in the toilets. I was crying and then slowly with a tail between my legs I tiptoed and sat next to her, outside the much feared room. I had never been in there. To this day I was just one of the oblivious mass in assembly. I was called in first and amongst sobs blurted out exactly what happened. The same sombre face that read the prayers in the morning announced,

"This is the day I will remember that Ann Leyfield forgot herself."

I left, never to have it mentioned again. But Linda did not get away so lightly. She had caused a usually obedient girl to lose her rag. Linda's parents were called in!

She had caused me years of worry and somehow after that she left me alone. She would even smile at me now and again. She told me once that her birthday came a day after mine and to this day on March 25th I say "Happy Birthday Linda, wherever you are."

After being in many school plays, choirs, writing for the magazine, I began to express myself more readily. In fact, Dad saw a difference. Once when I had answered him back for the first time he said,

"I don't know what they're teaching you at that grammar school. Have we done the right thing sending her there?" – Yes they had!

There was much that went over my head. I have vague memories of iron filings and *Michael Faraday*, litmus paper turning red, reciting French verbs and singing the school song in Latin. But I was being prepared for those important exams that would get me to a college so I could become a teacher. It happened, and it was thanks to my parents, my teachers and those that believed I could.

13. FOR THERE ARE THOSE THAT CARE

FOR THERE ARE THOSE THAT CARE

"Oh no, you're not still going? It's all God and skipping there! White gloves and black stockings – who d'you think you are?"

I couldn't answer my pal and ex-member. When I was seven I sat around a plastic toadstool singing, "Twit twit twoo." When I'd grown out of *Brownies* someone suggested the *Girls' Life Brigade* as there was no *Guides* group close by. At nine, I was submerged into a world of squad drill, hymn-singing, skipping tests and the idealism of purity and temperance.

We met every Friday in a small hall at the back of the Church of Christ, Derby Road, Gloucester. Today, rather new-looking red-brick flats stand where we sang, "I would be true for there are those that love me, I would be pure for there are those who care."

Perhaps I was always a "belonger" for I loved the extended care of the *GLB*. Miss M came each week to be our Captain. She was a short, suitably pure and kind person whom I so wished to please – in fact how could I let her down? She did care so much. She was a middle-aged spinster who dedicated her life to "her girls" and I was so proud to be one of them.

The *GLB* programme we often explained in our displays was to do with – SPES (Social, Physical, Educational and Spiritual Ideals.) Well, I felt it was rather heavily weighted on the Physical and Spiritual. We skipped, danced and marched to music provided by a lady as ancient as her candlesticked piano. She tinkled the same old tunes with a peppering of wrong notes. These routines were so drilled. I can still skip and march them!

Miss M was very proud of our new metal lock-up cupboard, which was full of our particular belongings, not to be used under any circumstances by the *Sunday School* or the *Children's Bright Hour*. In the bottom was a frayed cardboard box full of splitting old daps which the girls borrowed. There was a mustiness in that cupboard – a mixture of *Gloy* glue, passepartout, newly sharpened pencil crayons and the big dusty attendance book. In that book lay a history of faded names of girls of long ago, now married, moved away. Girls who had, just like me, heard a

13. FOR THERE ARE THOSE THAT CARE

hundred Devotionals, taken yearly Scripture examinations and learnt PE exercises to music. These were the first keep fit classes I was to know.

I once went with the *GLB* to some celebration in the *Royal Albert Hall* and saw hundreds of girls doing "our" exercises. They also did swinging club routines with the lights off and the end of each club brightly illuminated. They drew a sparkling complex maze in the darkness. As a nine year old, what impressed me most were the opera glasses you could use from the red plush boxes, and the wonderful array of perfumes in the ladies' cloakroom. You could have a squirt of any if only you had the costly coin needed! It was a truly momentous occasion – the first time I had ever visited the capital and the first and only time a pigeon has landed on my head!

The *GLB* was chapel-based. No one seemed to mind that I was C of E as long as I attended their church once a month. In fact, if I didn't, I could lose my five points in the attendance book. On the other weeks we could gain our points in this way: 1 for wearing uniform; 1 for being punctual; 1 for church attendance; 1 for bringing subs (any amount would do) and 1 for good behaviour. For two years I won the silver cup at the prize giving for the highest marks. So proud I was to receive it but moaned every time the *Silvo* came out for me to clean it!

It was a strict routine and standards were kept high. I can remember Temperance exams where we quoted the sad tales of sportsmen who had bitten the dust and I could recite percentage toxic levels of alcohol in their bloodstream. I vowed with such determination never to break my pledge to ban the demon drink!

We were rather go-ahead in learning DIY skills. Still in *GLB* at the tender age of sixteen, the only man, apart from the Minister, entered our hall to teach us how to wire a plug or change a washer on a tap. It was the only test I failed – not that it was hard – but I was so very aware of the soft voiced young man, who smelt of just-bathed carbolic and had smooth trimmed fingernails. I remember admiring his hands, so very different to my own Dad's railwayman's hands ingrained in black soot from the line. He was only too aware of my open stare, so much so he walked me home from Church Parade. After an awkward silence he asked me if I would like to see his new electric keyboard. Somehow in my crisp uniform and pure white gloves, it was unseemly to accept. I dithered a polite refusal which I was to regret for many a day.

It was the pride of the uniform which made you sit up straight and gave you a privilege in belonging. We wore it to our Annual rallies at the beautiful Cowley Manor. It was there we met all the other Gloucestershire companies and an army of officials who proudly gave us white-gloved salutes and approving nods as we marched and skipped, sang and prayed.

Miss M was no tell-tale. At Cowley she never told of our midnight feast. On her torch patrol she avoided opening the door. She knew we would talk and giggle for hours, munching apples and fruit cake under the sheets. The next night we would often plan a feast but somehow these never happened as we were often asleep before the wall lights were dimmed.

I was to be a *GLB* girl for nine years and when I was eighteen I left home to go to college. Perhaps it was well timed as the *Girls' Life Brigade* was to become the *Girls' Brigade*, with a new and very different uniform I found hard to accept. My old uniform was washed and sent back to Miss M but this time it would not be passed on to another girl. The blue dress was being replaced by a white

13. FOR THERE ARE THOSE THAT CARE

shirt and navy skirt and an *RAF* type hat. The *Brigade* was changing. It was the beginning of a new era.

Several years later I visited Derby Road and the company were meeting, the same as ever, on a Friday night. Miss M was still there, the new girls were so young, so eager and many different nationalities. The same old lady sat at the same piano. She told me nowadays girls just don't have the respect – I remembered she'd said that when I was there. Miss M, although a little greyer still had that gentle, yet firm approach I was to try and imitate in my own teaching later. How I admired the way she made each girl feel so very important. We were the children she had never had. We were her pride for the future to become reliable good wives, and loving mothers.

It is with the turning of decades the messages and hopes have stayed. I look back and I'm grateful for all of the "Miss M"s in my life, for indeed I have always been so fortunate in that there were those who cared.

BUT AM I GOOD ENOUGH?

When I was six, a young woman with dark straight hair knocked on our door. She told Mum and Dad that she went to All Saints Church. She asked if she could take us children to *Sunday School*. Mum and Dad had both attended *Sunday School* as children, but were not regular church goers. After much consideration, Dad said we could go as long as no pressure would be put on us. So that was how I was introduced to the church.

I had been christened at All Saints and it was to the same church I went to *Sunday School*. It was in a back room with a grand piano. Each week we were given a sticker for our stamp book. I hated it if we didn't go, as there would be an ugly space in my book. I remember having bear-skinned mittens for a present and dropping one down the outside church toilet. I didn't tell anyone and hid the spare one. But I knew God would know as it was in His toilet!

All Saints had a "daughter church" called The Church of the Good Shepherd. It was in Derby Road. They needed children for the choir, so by the time I was seven I was regularly attending Communion, Evensong and choir practice on a Wednesday. John was also in the choir and Roger wore the much respected red robe of an altar server.

I soon learnt the service responses by heart but didn't really understand their importance as I skipped and recited the Creed. I was forever humming hymns from *Ancient and Modern*. I enjoyed being part of the Good Shepherd family especially when Mum came to a service and then I would sing extra loudly.

When I was thirteen it was decided that I should be confirmed. I went back to All Saints for my training. I don't remember what we learnt, only that I became more and more concerned as to whether I was good enough to take part in such an honour. I borrowed Mum's prayer book that she had had on her confirmation. I copied out prayers on best paper and put them by my bed. With knees on hard, cold lino I recited long confessions of terrible sins. These sins were just the same as any other twelve year old, but nevertheless they worried me. Mum was concerned. She asked why I was writing out these long prayers. I said I didn't know.

The big day came: March 26th 1963 and I was confirmed at St Paul's Church by the Bishop of Gloucester. There were children from several churches. I stood with the All Saints children. A lady from their congregation gave them all a white prayer book. I didn't get one as I was from the daughter church. It didn't matter that I felt special in my white dress because Mum was so upset I didn't receive a prayer book like the others. She said it was typical of how the two churches did not mix. At an early age I was introduced to church politics!

The first Sunday afterwards I was to receive my first communion. The vicar, lay preacher, the choir master and

14. BUT AM I GOOD ENOUGH?

all the congregation knew it was my special day. It was also Mum's birthday. When it came to the part in the service when I had to receive Communion I froze in the choir stall. I couldn't move. I put my head down and cried. After the service Mum was not pleased. When the kindly vicar asked me why I had not gone up to the altar rail I sobbed, "I'm not good enough."

I also went to another church, once a month. This was a Baptist church that was linked with my *Girls' Life Brigade* group. It was to attend their Church Brigade. I preferred their jolly songs and their sermons were not of fear and retribution, with God waiting for you to fail. Theirs was a fatherly God who I felt more comfortable with.

Choir was becoming more interesting. A young man called Malcolm was the new organist. He wore smart suits and went to the cathedral private school. He spoke with a polished accent and I loved his dark eyes. I began singing, "I want to be Malcolm's girl." He didn't notice me. I was too young for him and he started to date one of the older girls. John went on holiday with his family and both sets of parents became close friends. Malcolm was always just a friend but I did have my dreams of what might have happened, if I had been a few years older…

I continued in the choir for many years until I went to college when I was eighteen. The many services, sermons and caring parishioners made their mark and eventually have given me a structure that I no longer fear. Mum often said I was too sensitive. Certainly odd comments and actions have made a huge impact on my decisions in life. If that young woman hadn't stopped at my house and asked to take us to church, my life could have been very different. I'm very grateful she came.

I have not always been a regular church goer. I haven't always prayed. But, when life later became very difficult to bear, I found it natural to pray. I was carried through those times. No matter how bad things were I have always found something I could thank God for.

Post Script

Many years later I told the story of not receiving the first communion to a kind vicar called Val Turner. She said, "I want to apologise for the way you were treated. By the way, no one is good enough. We're all sinners, and for sinners, Jesus waits at the altar with arms open wide." These words made things clear and I wrote a song called "*With Arms open Wide.*" It was recorded with eight other tracks and to date has raised almost £1000 for charity.

AN EASTER I ONCE KNEW

"Get the two dozen I ordered. Don't squash them and no nibbling. You never know who'll drop in after Church."

With a warm half crown in my hand, I waited outside the corner baker's shop for the hot cross buns. I remember now the warm spicy smell as I waited in the queue. The window was no longer full of loaves and doughnuts – only mountains of hot cross buns and a few sedate marzipan covered simnel cakes and flat currant Easter biscuits. We knew that our favourite shop would reverently close by noon in respect of the day, for Good Friday was a sombre occasion with businesses closed and no school, only a stark morning service of remembrance.

I was in the choir and on this day felt peeved at only being able to wear my black surplice and hat. The white jabot was being laundered and starched for the big day to come. The flowerless bare altar was cold and unwelcoming. As I sang softly of "a green hill far away," I dreamed of squashy hot cross buns waiting at home.

We had ogled the eggs in the newsagents for weeks, with our noses squashed against the window. By Easter Saturday only the largest were left, still shining with silvery wrap and satin bows to treasure. On this day we would hard boil our breakfast eggs, and then decorate them ready for Easter tea. There would be a tinkling in jam jars and much mixing on saucers to get the right colours to paint intricate flower designs and nursery Humpties. They would be arranged proudly waiting for their time.

A couple of cards would have arrived in the post. They would not be opened until the next day. Each year Auntie Alice and Uncle Bill and Aunty Ginny would send their Easter wishes. The cards showed the familiar pictures of churches and spring blossoms and the gold embossed crosses could be felt through the envelope. They would stand by the bowl of hyacinths which had been stored in a dark cupboard during the winter months, and now stood waiting in pride of place on the mantelpiece.

Church bells woke us on Easter day, and wearing our brightest and prettiest spring outfits we went to Church. Some ladies would wear floppy pale felt hats with satin bands. Once, a proud lady even wore crimson artificial cherries around her Easter bonnet. We giggled at the choir boy who stood behind her and pretended to pick them. I would wear my stiff, starched white jabot and it would rub my neck as we marched in a long procession around the church. I would sing loudly for all to hear because it was my brother, Roger who had led us carrying the large, brass, processional cross.

The altar had been transformed in shining glory of white and gold. There were vases laden with white arum lilies. Each bloom was special as these had been ordered by parishioners, weeks before. At a certain time in the service the vicar would read out from a scroll a list of names of

15. AN EASTER I ONCE KNEW

the "dearly departed." My gran was one of these and when he called her name my mum's eyes would fill with tears, and I would search amongst the blooms wondering which was in remembrance of her – we never did take it home.

After all the hallelujahs, the service over, this was what we had been waiting for – Easter eggs! They were beautiful, but soon lost their promise as great caverns were munched out. I used one pointed side of the egg to draw cartoon ducks on the other. I used the cardboard cut outs to draw egg shapes with huge bows. I was once given a chocolate rabbit, delicately engraved with life-like fur and tall pointed ears. I ate its head and was so saddened by the stumpy hollow feet that were left. I tried hard to stuff the silver rabbit cover with plasticine to recreate my lost bunny, but he looked mangled and twisted. I vowed that day never to eat a chocolate rabbit again.

The eggs we had painted were now smashed and we ate the multi-coloured flesh mashed into sandwiches for tea. Feeling tired and a little queasy, I sold my remaining chocolate eggshells to my brother John for nine pence each. I decided to keep the little bags of *Chocolate Buttons* and *Smarties* for all the ordinary days which lay ahead, with dreadful things such as school and piano lessons when a few old squashed sweets in your sticky pocket could help you on your way.

PINK CHRISTMAS BELLS

"We'll have to chop the top off. It just won't fit in. Don't put it close to the walls. We don't want to mark the paper and be viewing that all year. I don't know why we still have one – they make such a mess, needles dropping all over the mat. Get some of that Christmas wrap to put round the bucket. Get it near the plug for the lights. Oh I know they always go out, but perhaps they won't this year."

We all smiled, knowing that they did always go out – generally on Christmas Eve when the shops had just shut. My brother John and I would be hovering with the dusty brown box from the attic. We knew that under the yellowed paper telling news long gone were the magical trimmings which were part of our Christmas.

To others they were just some faded glass balls, old metal candle holders, hand-made paper chains, concertina-shaped Chinese lanterns, milk-bottle top decorations and lastly a set of pink plastic bells. When you brushed past the tree they would tinkle out of tune. This sound was as much part of Christmas as the *Salvation Army* band playing in Gloucester's King's Square or *Bing Crosby*'s *White Christmas*. To me, the pink bells were just always there.

It was a hopeful time. As a young child it began weeks before as I wished while stirring the Christmas pudding and vowed that this year I would be the one to bite into the silver sixpence. In later years I would gaze up at the mistletoe and dream of the pleasure of a stolen kiss from my brother's friend – who was quite unaware of my hopes. As we looked into the orange glow of a winter's fire, we would dream of Christmas surprises.

There is one I remember vividly. I had seen a small, cheap, bright work-basket in *Woolworths*. It was woven plastic and a garish pink. It contained thin weak thread and needles with the tiniest of eyes. I had expressed to Mum my absolute devotion to this thing of beauty. She had said wouldn't I prefer a stronger one of a better quality, woven in cane but my heart was set on the plastic box. To my delight I unwrapped it on Christmas morning.

There were always the three white pillowcases labelled, Roger, John and Ann at the bottom of my parents' big bed. Mum and Dad were smiling dozily as the three of us piled each new thing in front of them. We unveiled each new present just as if they didn't already know. I often had a doll or a tea-set. My brothers had *Meccano* or a *Hornby* clockwork train set. There was always a selection box, a comic annual, a treasured tangerine, chocolate money and a white sugar mouse.

After Family Communion where we sang the same carols as we always had, we came back for Christmas dinner. It was often a large chicken my grandfather had fattened for us at his home in Herefordshire. One year we had gone to collect the bird and Grandad said this year it would be very fresh, in fact it was still alive – a large turkey. Hiding in the

16. PINK CHRISTMAS BELLS

outhouse I heard the bird squawking as it ran for its life. I saw Grandad grab it by its neck and the cruel cleaver fall on the chopping block. My brother John teased me by whispering, "Gobble, gobble" as we went home in the car. He even whispered, "Gobble, gobble," as Dad brought in the well-browned bird ready to be carved. That afternoon the dinner lost some of its savour and I had to fill up with Christmas pud instead!

Like most families we had our traditions and each year our own Christmas stories were retold. Mum would say,

"Remember when our Ann was Mary in the Infant's play? There she was, all serene and loving singing, *We Will Rock You* then she calmly walks out leaving the baby Jesus doll. Off-stage she realises what she's done then rushes back on, grabs Jesus by the leg and drags him out showing his bare plastic bottom to the world!"

"D'you remember when our Ann was singing a solo verse of *Away in a Manger* in church? I was so proud till she started swaying like young ones do and soon all the front line was too – John whispered, 'They're on a boat!' Well that was it – how we stifled our giggles I don't know, and our Ann looking as holy as the vicar made it worse!"

To this day the accumulation of Christmas tales and traditions has continued, but I remember one year when everything marked time for me. It was the first year I no longer had my Mum and Dad. My husband and young baby were of course precious, but somehow the hub of my wheel was missing – it felt incomplete. I had inherited a couple of pink plastic bells from my childhood trees and these lay unused at the bottom of the box.

As the years passed my little boy held the same excitement over our cardboard box full of Christmas trimmings. One year he pulled out the pink plastic bells – their tinkle still off key brought back with a rush all the warmth and excitement of my Christmas past. I sat him on my knee and started to tell him all my Christmas stories.

Each year since then, new memories have been made and old ones relived. As I recognised the hope and excitement in his young eyes my wheel once more became complete. Once again the pink Christmas bells will tinkle out of tune on this year's tree.

FIRST LOVE

This was it. He was there, next to me, practically rubbing shoulders, squashed behind a till of a department store's *Toy Fayre* in Gloucester. It was Christmas Eve 1965. The rush was over and I had been asked to cash up with him.

His name was Peter. I'd watched him for weeks demonstrating on his hands and knees the wind-ups, amusing the children, charming the old ladies – but we'd never been this close. I was counting the three penny bits, hands all a tremble – I even forgot how many made a shilling, just went on counting until he stared at the toppling coins.

I followed him out of the building to see which bus he caught in King's Square. I could get home on that one too, so I plonked myself next to him, grinning and gawping. He asked where I lived. I gave a vague reply. I'd already missed my stop as I didn't want my journey to end. I had to get off. It was so far out of my way, but then he looked at me and asked my name. He wished me "Happy Christmas" and smiled. I tip-toed from that bus, not feeling the rain; not caring that I was at least a mile from home – he had noticed me. He had said my name.

At fifteen the first flicker of a powerful fire had ignited all my senses. I was whirled into a new dimension where the focus was so sharp and real and just for me. Every thing to do with Peter was vital; all the rest was in a mist of dullness and indifference. I wanted to shout from the top of Painswick Beacon, "I love Peter!" – I didn't of course; instead I inked his initials indelibly on my school satchel. Never again would Peter be an ordinary name.

He came to my home and was accepted by everyone.

"He fits in, one of the family – such a nice boy" my mum had said, and for twenty two months and fourteen days I could say Peter was my boyfriend – well so I thought.

I had got over the disappointment of the tight hard-lipped first kiss. I think it was a first venture for both of us, perfunctory and dutiful. He would play darts with my brothers and I would write poems about him. He would watch television with my family, tease mum and make her giggle. I composed songs about him, he would never hear. Each time he went home, the evening had the sealed stamp of the brief good night kiss.

"He's only a child, enjoys the company. Don't stare at him so. He comes to see your brothers as much as you."

Mum's comments stung hard. She could see the let down coming. It was a shock to me.

"Twenty two months with the same girl – you'll have to marry her!"

It was thanks to this comment from his pal that Peter

17. FIRST LOVE

changed. Kindly he finished regular meetings, taking my world and obliterating it. I wrote to him, begging him, but he said it was the end.

"Show him!" my friends said and Julie and I attended the Saturday Guildhall dances. With bright lights flashing and our bare feet around a heap of handbags, I twisted the hours away letting *The Beatles'* music pierce through the hurt. If I half closed my eyes and sang with the singer, I could be just like one of *Pan's People* – slim, attractive and the boy at the microphone was singing only for me. He knew how I felt.

In a full to the brim whirl of dances, leaning in the record booths to soak up the latest 45s, coffee in the *Wimpy Bar* – I was at least busy. But nothing could soothe the scars, or fill the empty hole he had left, especially at night in the desperate moments before sleep conquered memory.

"*The Next Time*" *Cliff Richard* sang to me and there was a change just round the corner, a new boy, so different. He was not happy-go-lucky like Peter, but serious and deep. I couldn't understand Mum's concern about him. It was the fact that he wanted to be alone with me that worried her the most. She moaned about us "burning hours of electricity in the front room." I felt that her worries were more than just bills.

One day she stole enough courage to say to me that she had something very important to say. Painfully and very deliberately she whispered,

"A boy may try but a girl must deny!"

She then walked away leaving me bewildered and somewhat amused when I realised I had just had my "Birds and bees" talk!

77

As time went on whenever we met neighbours or Mum's friends, she would say, "Girls are such a worry. You do hope they won't bring their troubles home."

I couldn't see what ever this had to do with me!

Strangely I think Peter missed my family and, when I wasn't there, he sometimes visited my mum for a chat. He sent me birthday and Christmas cards but we didn't meet. Even years later when I was living away at college I received a postcard saying, "Wondered who to send this to, love Peter." By then my head was turned by someone new. Peter and I met once and I told him I was getting married. From then on there were no cards, no visits, and I felt a loss that surprised me.

The years have changed into decades and I still wonder at the extreme power of those heightened moments when life was so vital, so sharp, so dreadful, and so wonderful. At the time I could not imagine how those feelings could change. But, in growing up I had to say goodbye to so many things that could no longer belong.

Most of the time I am a million miles from these thoughts, but it only takes an old song on the radio and immediately I am fifteen again and I am running to meet him at the door. But I no longer can get burnt by first love, I can just smile and toast in the memory of its warmth.

THE LADIES FROM STATIONERY

One of Mum's sayings was "You can't put old heads on young shoulders." This story took place when I was just fifteen years old and a lesson was painfully learnt.

I hated waiting for my turn at the hatch. I just stood there outside Personnel with all the other Saturday assistants waiting to see Old Man Chivers. At nine o'clock he would open his hatch door and tell us which department we had to go to.

It all seemed so pointless as we were sent to the same each week – Spotty long legs to DIY; High heels and wiggle to perfumery; Frizzy frump to top floor restaurant and poor, poor Ida with a droopy eyelid and gappy mouth to the lowest of the low – Staff Canteen.

I had been warned at my interview that appearance was important, so in neat black uniform with a white lace collar I was sent to Miss Fairbourn and Miss Childs at Stationery. They had been working at that same department for over twenty years.

"How old are you girl?"

"Fifteen, almost sixteen"

"Which school did you attend?"

I told her.

"Ah Miss Childs, at last Personnel are sending us grammar school material. Now put your bag in that drawer and watch me."

It took almost a whole morning to train me how to approach and deal with a customer. I was told to hover, take interest but not to intervene until directly approached, then smile and a quiet, "Can I help you madam?" when taking the money, not to put out one's hand until the customer was ready, and when approaching the new electric till to be cautious as it was annoyingly unpredictable. In all operations one stood well back.

All notes were to be put in a special holder and I was to check change and count it back into the customer's hand. Each item and receipt must be placed in a paper bag large enough to fold over. The transaction complete, then a gentle smile and retiring thank you. On no account was I to lean or lounge over the counter, as this was slovenly and clothes could easily be snagged on the paper hooks. I was not to stand obscured behind the large sale placards and any complaints were to be dealt with only by the department head – The Stationery Buyer.

18. THE LADIES FROM STATIONERY

I was sent to tidy the card shelves, sort out pens, arrange sets of envelopes and by the end of the day I felt my legs would never hold out. I saw a small stool in the corner and thought "I'll just sit for a moment."

"Are you ill, girl?"

"No Miss Fairbourn."

"Perhaps she feels faint?"

"No thank you Miss Childs."

"Then get up and never sit again!"

I was sent each week to Stationery. The ladies gave me a special store name – "Miss Lent". After several weeks they softened towards me. I began to think they were really fond of me. Miss Fairbourn said I had great promise, especially now that they had "polished and smoothed out" my "rough edges."

I found I began to take on their slow reserved speech and efficient walk. I began to polish my nails and hold my head high. They no longer called me "Miss Lent", it was "Our Miss Lent." I was so proud to be a lady from Stationery.

One Saturday, Old man Chivers was not there and a new man met us at the hatch. When my turn came he said, "Report to Staff Canteen."

To my horror I started to stutter stupidly.

"But I always go to Stationery."

"Ida Rawlings is absent. They're short staffed. Report to Staff Canteen."

I cannot explain the degree of humiliation I felt when putting on the silly hat and Ida's pink overall – too short in the sleeve, gravy stained and with "Staff Canteen" emblazoned all over the splitting pocket.

The rest of the crew were kind to me. They did not seem to notice me biting my lip or the tear filled eyes as my manicured nails picked at the dregs in the plug hole covered with brown slimy water. They tried to make the day interesting by giving me interesting jobs to do. Instead of "Miss Lent" I became "Dearie" or "Lovie," and although I prayed Ida would soon be back, things were not really that bad.

We sat separately to have tea, all pink overalls together. Some told jokes. The laughter seemed too loud. After I was sent to clear plates from the far row, and there were Miss Fairbourn and Miss Childs finishing their afternoon scone. They saw me and stared. How I hated my tight pink overall and lopsided hat. I took a deep breath and with head held high I resumed my "stationery walk."

"Good afternoon Miss Fairbourn.
 Good afternoon Miss Childs."

They very deliberately turned their heads away. I took their plates. No word was spoken. I was not their "Miss Lent" anymore.

When I got home I vowed I would never return to the store, but the following Saturday I was back at the hatch. Old man Chivers was back and sent me back to Stationery. I do not know what I expected, but the ladies greeted me as if nothing had happened. No one mentioned the Saturday before. Work went on the same as ever, but I had changed. I would never forget the eyes that looked away.

(The names of the characters have been changed)

ALWAYS THERE – MY MUM

Sometimes when the winds of life blow too hard and strip me of all pretension I am once more a child running to her outstretched arms, my tear-stained cheek is pressed against her, smelling her soapy warmth, and with eyes shut I am saved – no-one can hurt me now – my mum is here.

It wasn't the words she said or the stroking of my hair, she knew how bad things could seem, she knew how much I needed her. Sometimes my older brothers would argue and tease, drive her to distraction. She'd say "I can't stand it any more... right! I'm going." She'd march up the back alley and slam the door. The act was lost on the boys – they knew she'd never really go – but I would run, crying, shouting, and she, hiding behind the door, could bear it no longer and she would stalk back, head held high, giving us "just one more chance" yet again.

She'd been brought up a country girl, in service, and later became a cook in a large household. Her favourite television programme was *Upstairs Downstairs* – she said "that's just how it was". Because of this background she taught us sayings like "Know your place", "Show respect". My father was not brought up in service but believed in the worth of the individual. I followed in Dad's footsteps and it saddened me to see Mum's humble reverence when speaking to the doctor, vicar, headmaster or anyone she considered "of position".

"Real gentry can mix with all sorts without putting on airs" said Dad, "as long as you're honest you can look anyone in the eye." He proved this the day he went to *Buckingham Palace* to see my brother receive his *Duke of Edinburgh*'s gold award. Mum just said she couldn't cope, but true to Dad's fashion he's there in all the photos, smiling proud with Roger, as if he'd passed it himself.

Railwayman's pay was poor, even with overtime, so when I was nine years old Mum started work at a uniform factory where she snipped the threads left by the machinists. They'd had their chairs taken away, supposedly to make them work more and chat less. Mum had swollen ankles and coughed from the machine dust. She'd whisper to Dad about her boss. He'd say "Pack it in girl," but she never did. I was to remember her tiredness when later I went to college. Just to get me there, Mum had worked hard, so I had to do well and not let her down.

She didn't say a great deal, she was a doer and her actions shaped and coloured our lives in a way I later learned that not all families enjoyed.

19. ALWAYS THERE – MY MUM

At Christmas time the little extra traditions were created and upheld by Mum. There were routines of typical Sunday treats or holidays. She had a great feeling for family tradition. She once said to me,

"Don't ever fall out with your brothers. Family's important, we've all got to stick together – there's none so sad as families who don't get on."

This was her whole philosophy, even if you bit back what you thought, you were always pleasant to everyone, kept your problems to yourself.

I didn't really know her problems. I knew often after a lunch she'd say:

"I'm just putting me head down."

Her arms folded on the table, she'd shut her eyes and have a rest. We went on playing round her chair, but she escaped into herself for a moment. Then after what seemed to me a lifetime of waiting she'd say "This won't do", wash her face with cold water from the brass tap then she would boil up some more water for the washing-up.

"Always do your best: work hard in school. One day you'll be someone in life", she'd say – I felt I always was someone and it saddened me that she felt she wasn't.

Later she did cleaning at a local college – she would "do" for one of the lecturers in hall. It was back to service again for her and in a way it maddened me – I didn't want her cleaning for someone.

"But the money comes in," she would reassure me, "and Miss R's all right."

I remember my first teaching salary at twenty one. Mum's eyes welled with pride as she said "Look Vic, she's earning almost twice your basic!" – and I felt ashamed knowing he'd worked thirty years on the line while I had taught for only one month.

Praise wasn't given often; in fact it was rarely given in words – more a smile, admiring glance or a squeeze of your hand. It was the warmth of all the gestures of love – like the piece of cold toast wrapped for my break at school each day, when she knew I watched the girl down the road eat her *Mars* bar.

"One day we'll buy our own home and it won't be soon if it's frittered away on niceties," she would say.

Chocolate belonged only to Easter time, or a Christmas selection box, or presented with a bunch of daffs on Mothering Sunday.

"People who waste their money on sweets and posh clothes will never afford to buy their own places. One day we will – even on a railwayman's pay."

And she was right. Mum and Dad would nod, united in their decisions. Perhaps they did disagree, but never in front of us, they were the rule makers and nothing would alter them.

At the end of every day she always had the same goodnight routine, even if we'd been chased upstairs with Dad threatening,

"Just wait till I get my hands on you!"

Once, as an adult, when life had become too much I went to my parent's new, and paid for, bungalow and burst into

19. ALWAYS THERE – MY MUM

tears. Mum said to stay the night and I was glad to do so. Although I was all grown now, she still made me a milky drink, tucked me in, pulled the blankets under my chin and kissed forehead goodnight. And I once more was like the child running to her opened arms – I could shut my eyes and feel safe; no one could hurt me, as Mum was there.

Mum died some years ago, and when I became a mum, I wondered why sometimes I didn't feel as grown up and sure of things as I'd always felt a mum should be. I know now why she needed the rests from our idle chatter during the day. I know now the sorts of worries the adults whispered about. When I have tucked my own child in at bedtime, in the same way as she did, I always felt her nearness and her warmth. When that wind has blown too hard for me: once more I have felt she was always there.

20. MY DAD – A MAN OF FEW WORDS

MY DAD – A MAN OF FEW WORDS

Sometimes in the dark sinking moments before I drift off to sleep, I think I hear the catch on the old back gate again, the sound of his turning cycle wheels scooting down the back alley. There's the hollow clumping of his boots on the wooden floor of the shed as he puts the bike away and then the rattling handle of the back door, and his voice calling out, "Any one at 'ome?" and I would lie listening from my bed, warmed and complete to know that Dad had finished his shift.

If he'd been on earlies he'd arrive home tired and hungry. We kids soon learnt to keep out of his way as he took off his canvas haversack and heavy railwayman's coat. He'd turn up his check shirt sleeves and lather his arms in a chipped enamel bowl. No one would speak as Mum put the dinner in front of him and poured a cup of tea. I would watch from behind the sofa until he'd pushed the scraped pudding bowl away and then there would be all the questions:

"Dad, if I could save all my money d'you think I could have..." or "Dad, you'll never guess what happened in school today…"

Mum would smile and Dad would nod and I would come from behind my hiding hole and take my place on his knee and his large hands would encircle me and I was in safe harbour from all the perils of the day.

He was a strong powerful man with an awesome temper. When my brothers drove him to the end of his tether he would shake with rage. He would be red and speechless. It was not like him to discuss or chat – he would listen to all the fors and againsts and then as an overseeing judge, pronounce the verdict and no one could alter it.

Thrift and regular saving was a way of life as he wanted to own our rented house. He didn't believe in banks and cheques. Cash was put in the building society and a hundred pounds was kept in a box in the roof, rather like the half bottle of brandy, only to be used in an emergency.

Straightforward, black and white were his views. He was a staunch *Labour* man, who was bluntly honest and like the Aunt in the poem, *Matilda*, "kept a strict regard for truth." One of his creeds drummed in to us children was "Know what is your own." He had no time for easy credit. Buy now pay later was for him a fool's choice.

Although we feared our father's wrath and learnt to keep out of his way when he was tired, in retrospect, there was a closeness and utter reliability because he was the figurehead of the family – solid as a rock and always there. He had little formal education but I would rank him as one of the wisest men I've ever known - perhaps in the way he dealt with the trials life served him.

20. MY DAD – A MAN OF FEW WORDS

I'll never forget the day my brother John borrowed Dad's one and only, well-loved, hardly-used car and dented it in a crash. John came in white and trembling and sobbed the news to Dad. I cowered, waiting for the temper to erupt, but instead he spoke with a gentle voice and showed only concern for John, then calmly took over. This I found in later disasters was his strength. Mum went into dithering pieces in an emergency. He took on a powerful calm and quietly dealt with the situation.

Only once did I see this amazing power weaken. It was the night my mother died. We all knew she was dying. Dad was comforting her and talking about all the wonderful holidays and happy times they'd had together, then a little later the drip to her arm stopped and it was over. His voice wavered in hysterical disbelief. He just wouldn't believe me that she had died. It was then somehow my arms became strong and held him as a child to me.

Without Mum, Dad was lost, but kept his despair behind shut doors of their dream bungalow that they'd saved for. He was not used to fending for himself and bravely learnt to cook and clean and iron his own shirts. My phone call at the end of the day was a poor substitute welcome home after a hard shift. I often wondered what were his memories as he waited on cold stations, or travelled the same endless lines alone in an uncomfortable guard's van.

91

For two years he was so very brave the way he carried on – keeping the garden and the house as if she were there. Even on the day he died he'd prepared the vegetables for his dinner before cycling to the doctor with a pain in his chest. He fell from his bike and was found dead by strangers. He was very special to us but at his funeral I realised how he had been admired by many. The small chapel was packed and the railwaymen's voices as they sang *Abide With Me* were rich and powerful – giving me strength for the day.

Clearing out all the mementos of the house, not a great deal was left to see apart from his savings and of course, the hundred pounds still in the box in the roof. I searched for personal things which were the essence of Dad. I found a few railwayman's diaries outlining shifts, his old school drawing books, *Sunday School* attendance sticker book, a *St John's Ambulance* medal, his *National Union of Railwaymen* badge, but also a large photograph album. The first pages show Dad as a boy standing on a chair and through the pages I found Dad's engagement to Mum, our christenings and lastly all the wonderful caravan holidays when he had no shifts to worry about and we had Dad completely to ourselves.

THE DAY THOU GAVEST

I peeped outside before closing the thick, lined, winter curtains. The day was fading fast and echoing in our ears was the last hymn of Evensong - *The Day Thou Gavest Lord Is Ended*. It was my favourite service. So few attended, often more in the choir than the handful on wooden seats of the congregation. The handful were special – wives of the lay preacher and the choir master, and a rather plump giggly lady in a fluffy hat with a rabbit's foot on it. She sat next to Mum and would openly look at her watch if the sermon was going on for too long! Then there was Mum, the most important person in the whole church. She wore a grey utility coat and a black velvet hat. Her eyes were cast down reverently, but in all her modesty she could not hide the pride she felt for her children in the choir.

After saying goodnight and receiving a hard handshake and an amiable thump on the back from the lay preacher, John and I would trip down the steps and wait for her. Then taking an arm each, we walked in harmony and chattered too much.

"Mum, who's on at the Palladium?
Russ Conway? *Alma Cogan*?"

"Only if we get you bathed on time! Dad's cleaned your shoes. They're laid out on newspaper in the scullery. Your dinner money is in the baccy tin with your savings money for your stamps. You can have cold toast in the morning for your break. And now, what have I got here?"

Eagerly we pushed out our palms for the *Fox*'s glacier mint left over from a car journey to grandad's. We only had sweets on car journeys. They stopped you mentioning the things we never mentioned. If you were sucking, your face couldn't turn green as you endured bumps and twists with the windows hardly ever opened.

Would there be crumpets for supper with *Ovaltine*? Crumpets tasted better if you were snuggled in a warm flannelette nightie, and munching as Dad rubbed your hair dry with a harsh hard towel, still rough and stiff from drying on the washing line.

Mum knew I longed to see *Russ Conway*. We had wooden arms on our chairs, and while he was playing, both my

21. THE DAY THOU GAVEST

hands were tripping over the wood, and it was me, not Russ who was playing. How I longed to play the piano. The longing would get me into scrapes at *Sunday School*. I would tinkle on the grand piano while the teacher was out of the room. Whether it was in the *Allington Hall* after a Beetle Drive or at school, I couldn't resist tinkling on the piano. I'd learnt to pick out a few nursery rhymes on my tiny pink *Pixiano* plastic, eight-noted piano that I'd been given for Christmas.

Then a wonderful thing happened. A neighbour's son had grown tired of his piano lessons. They would sell the piano to us and I could take over the lessons. The old walnut upright with brass candlesticks, and very much in need of repair, was wheeled up the road to take place in our front room. At the age of nine I began my formal music training and at 6:30 PM I had a music lesson, every Thursday evening for nine years!

My enthusiasm was often dampened by learning scales and examination pieces. Sometimes I wanted to give up but Mum said it would be a waste. She had heard that teachers would be more readily employed if they could play the piano. She was right and many years later I was in charge of music in the primary schools where I taught.

I started writing music of my own very early on. Once, when I was fifteen, I told my teacher that I had written a piece. She liked it and named it *Intermezzo*. She let me play it to an adult pupil.

"Who do you think wrote that?" she asked him.

"*Debussy*?" he replied.

I hadn't a clue who *Debussy* was but I was delighted to see my teacher laugh and assure me it was a huge compliment!

Many nights I sit at my piano and I am thrilled with its tone and beauty. It is as precious as it was many years ago. My husband bought it for me with his first teaching salary when we were not well off, but very happy. I still have an old *Ancient and Modern* hymn book and the yellowed pages are well thumbed by hundreds of parishioners who have found the number I know so well – 16, *The Day Thou Gavest Lord Is Ended*.

As I play and sing my favourite hymn, the light is fading fast. Mum is smiling from a faded photograph, everyone is settling down to a quiet evening and in my dreams I am marching, best foot forward, snuggling up to Mum's coat smelling of moth balls and cologne. We are chatting and she is nodding and her smile of pride is still there.

22. THE WEALTH OF PENNIES

THE WEALTH OF PENNIES

By the time I was thirty, Mum and Dad had died. They had prepared me for adult life.

As a child I used to believe I would somehow grow appropriately wise and mature as an adult. This wisdom would suddenly appear at about 20. I could then be relied upon to make good decisions!

"You can't put old heads on young shoulders," Mum often used to say knowingly.

As a young adult, Mum and Dad saw me make some seriously wrong decisions and could not interfere. They could no longer shield me.

I was later to experience the absolute ecstasy that life could give and also the depths of despair. Especially in the low times I have felt them very near. They would be waiting for me to find the important truth, honesty and love they had taught me to value. When I thought of what they would have said, the answer would become clearer.

They had given me a safe, structured and very loving childhood, peppered with simple warm memories. These memories are like pennies. I've gathered them and will always treasure them. They have given me my wealth.

22. THE WEALTH OF PENNIES

THE WEALTH OF PENNIES

I remember donkey days.
With regal back
I would view a perfect world
of waves to hurdle, sand to dig.
Sitting in a moulded car
with its bucket steering wheel,
I could zoom round the dunes
and be back for picnic treat
of gritty squashed sandwich and flat lemonade.

It would rain only at night
as we tightly sat round a table, playing cards.
With unfinished game, eyelids dropped.
Huddled in narrow bunks
the day dissolved into dreams
with the rhythm of raindrops on the caravan roof.

I remember Harvest days.
Sitting in a choir stall
viewing apples on artificial grass.
Of bread shaped into sheaves of corn
and Summer blooms a plenty
to adorn the proud produce
neatly laid, arranged with care,
and I could tell which marrow was ours.

22. THE WEALTH OF PENNIES

I remember frosty days.
Of ice-nipped fingers
warmed by coals glowing,
as hot chunks of bread were toasted
on a long twisted fork.

I remember being lifted out of a metal bath
engulfed with warm towel,
feeling as a princess wrapped in a stole,
then bustled with speed into night clothes,
leaving only small wet prints,
on a home made rug.

I remember crocus days.
Of counting buds
as they peel and shine
in my handkerchief plot of care.
Of squashed nose on shop window
gazing at eggs, as large as my head,
with satin bows to keep and treasure.

As seasons turn like pennies spinning,
each has but a short time to turn,
yet the brilliance of their form
and the memory of their movement
may fade, but never be lost.
For in their twists of time
I have found my wealth.

ACKNOWLEDGEMENTS

Several chapters from this book were originally published in *Cotswold Life* magazine, in the following editions:

- December 1991 — *My Dad, a Man of Few Words*
- March 1992 — *The Ladies from Stationery*
- April 1992 — *In a Slower Time*
- May 1992 — *The Ones Who Came to Call*
- July 1992 — *A Bit of Green*
- November 1992 — *Inside the Gate*
- December 1992 — *Pink Christmas Bells*
- April 1994 — *Food For Thought*
- February 1999 — *First Love*

In 2004 these autobiographical stories along with some new additions were compiled in an anthology published by the *Daily Mail*, which became the first edition of *A Wealth of Pennies*.

Cotswold Life published several more stories by Ann that are included in the collection *Let Me Tell You a Story*, now available worldwide on *Amazon, Kindle, Audible*, and from independent retail outlets.

Ann continued as a regularly commissioned writer for the magazine over eight years, also writing factual pieces, including the very first story for the premiere edition of sister publication *Your Cotswold Wedding*.

The publishers of this book wish to gratefully acknowledge *Cotswold Life*, *L&C Communications*, editors John Drinkwater, David B. MacDonald, and all who supported her writing career during this time.

A MUM OF MANY WORDS
Samuel Victor

When I was a child, my mum wrote a short story about her father, my grandfather Victor Leyfield, called *My Dad, a Man of Few Words*. This led to her being selected for a literature festival run by *The Times*, a tour of British libraries, and a string of published work in *Cotswold Life* magazine lasting eight years – each one would help fund another happy family getaway with my Dad in our small touring caravan.

Mum not only wrote autobiographical tales, but fiction, poetry, songs, musicals, technical workbooks and factual articles – as a child it was not uncommon for me to see her work in glossy magazines, newspapers, on BBC and ITV, to hear it played on the radio, or performed live. Unlike her Dad, she was a "Mum of *Many* Words" – and countless people have enjoyed them. This certainly inspired my own work in the media: acting, directing, animating, and writing films, books, comics and music.

I never got to meet her father – sadly he passed away just before I was born. When Mum told him that she thought she was pregnant, some of the last of his "few" words were "Nothing would make me happier". I wish we would have had a chance to meet, but everything that Mum told me about him over the years made me admire him greatly. When my agent told me that for professional purposes I would need to change my surname, I chose to repurpose my middle one, "Victor".

Growing up, we weren't rich, we weren't from London, we didn't have celebrity connections, but I watched Mum get success by just being creative and not being afraid to put herself out there – following her example has been the blueprint for my own career. She often donates profits from her ventures to charities and good causes, another great example that I follow. One area where we differ is that while I'm happy to shout about my achievements to all who will listen, Mum humbly downplays her talents. It's taken much persuading, but I'm so happy to have been able to help her get not one, but *four* full books published spanning her forty year career, preserved so that she will inspire people for generations to come, just as she's always done for me.

ABOUT THE AUTHOR

Ann Leyfield is a renowned writer whose work in poetry, prose and song have been regularly featured in British media since the 1980s (as Ann Jones), spanning television, radio, newspapers, books and magazines. A four-time selection for *The Times* and *The Sunday Times* Cheltenham Literature Festival through *Gloucestershire Writers' Network*, Ann also created the worldwide best-selling factual series of *Cracking the Code* books, several well loved children's musicals and her acclaimed autobiography *A Wealth of Pennies* was first published through the *Daily Mail*.

ALSO FROM THE AUTHOR
Further publications in this series, from Victorious MCG

LET ME TELL YOU A STORY
An Anthology of the Stories I Love to Share
ISBN: 9798873595952

EVERY POEM HAS A STORY
Snapshots of a Lifetime Distilled into Verse
ISBN: 9798872897187

SONGS TO MAKE A DIFFERENCE
Christian Songs and the Stories That Gave Them Life
ISBN: 9798873597192

Available worldwide on Amazon, Kindle, Audible, and independent retail outlets.

Printed in Great Britain
by Amazon